Socialism: Positive and Negative

by Robert Rives La Monte

PREFACE

Of the papers in this little volume two have appeared in print before: "Science and Socialism" in the International Socialist Review for September, 1900, and "Marxism and Ethics" in Wilshire's Magazine for November, 1905. My thanks are due to the publishers of those periodicals for their kind permission to re-print those articles here. The other papers appear here for the first time.

There is an obvious inconsistency between the treatment of Materialism in "Science and Socialism" and its treatment in "The Nihilism of Socialism." I would point out that seven years elapsed between the composition of the former and that of the latter essay. Whether the inconsistency be a sign of mental growth or deterioration my readers must judge for themselves. I will merely say here that the man or woman, whose views remain absolutely fixed and stereotyped for seven years, is cheating the undertaker. What I conceive the true significance of this particular change in opinions to be is set forth in the essay on "The Biogenetic Law."

Some Socialists will deprecate what may seem to them the unwise frankness of the paper on "The Nihilism of Socialism." To them I can only say that to me Socialism has always been essentially a revolutionary movement. Revolutionists, who attempt to maintain a distinction between their exoteric and their esoteric teachings, only succeed in making themselves ridiculous. But, even were the maintenance of such a distinction practicable, it would, in my judgment, be highly inexpedient. As a mere matter of policy, ever since I first entered the Socialist Movement, I have been a firm believer in the tactics admirably summed up in Danton's "De l'audace! Puis de l'audace! Et toujours de l'audace!"

Should any reader find himself repelled by "The Nihilism of Socialism," let me beg that he will not put the book aside until he has read the essay on "The Biogenetic Law."

I do not send forth this little book with any ambitious hope that it will be widely read, or even that it will convert any one to Socialism. My hope is far more modest. It is that this book may be of some real service, as a labor-saving device, to the thinking men and women who have felt the lure of Socialism, and are trying to discover just what is meant by the oft-used words 'Marxian Socialism,' Should it prove of material aid to even one such man or woman, I would feel that I had been repaid a hundred-fold for my labor in writing it.

ROBERT RIVES LA MONTE. Feb. 7, 1907.

TABLE OF CONTENTS

SCIENCE AND SOCIALISM[1]

(International Socialist Review, September, 1900.)

Until the middle of this (the nineteenth) century the favorite theory with those who attempted to explain the phenomena of History was the Great-Man-Theory. This theory was that once in a while through infinite mercy a great man was sent to the earth who yanked humanity up a notch or two higher, and then we went along in a humdrum way on that level, or even sank back till another great man was vouchsafed to us. Possibly the finest flower of this school of thought is Carlyle's Heroes and Hero Worship. Unscientific as this theory was, it had its beneficent effects, for those heroes or great men served as ideals, and the human mind requires an unattainable ideal. No man can be or do the best he is capable of unless he is ever reaching out toward an ideal that lies beyond his grasp. Tennyson put this truth in the mouth of the ancient sage who tells the youthful and ambitious Gareth who is eager to enter into the service of King Arthur of the Table Round:

"-----------the King Will bind thee by such vows as is a shame A man should not be bound by, yet the which No man can keep."

This function of furnishing an ideal was performed in former times by these great men and more especially by those great men whom legend, myth and superstition converted into gods. But with the decay of the old faiths the only possible fruitful ideal left is the ideal upheld by Socialism, the ideal of the Co-operative Commonwealth in which the economic conditions will give birth to the highest, purest, most altruistic ethics the world has yet seen. It is true the co-operative commonwealth is far more than a Utopian ideal, it is a scientific prediction, but at this point I wish to emphasize its function as an ideal.

But it is obvious that this Great Man theory gave no scientific clue to history. If the Great Man was a supernatural phenomenon, a gift from Olympus, then of course History had no scientific basis, but was dependent upon the arbitrary caprices of the Gods, and Homer's Iliad was a specimen of accurate descriptive sociology. If on the other hand the great man was a natural phenomenon, the theory stopped short half way toward its goal, for it gave us no explanation of the genesis of the Great Man nor of the reasons for the superhuman influence that it attributed to him.

Mallock, one of the most servile literary apologists of capitalism, has recently in a book called "Aristocracy and Evolution" attempted to revive and revise this theory and give it a scientific form. He still attributes all progress to Great Men, but with the brutal frankness of modern bourgeois Capitalism, gives us a new definition of Great Men. According to Mallock, the great man is the man who makes money. This has long been the working theory of bourgeois society, but Mallock is the first of them who has had the cynicism or the stupidity to confess it. But mark you, by this confession he admits the truth of the fundamental premise of modern scientific socialism, our Socialism, viz., that the economic factor is the dominant or determining factor in the life of society. Thus you see the ablest champion of bourgeois capitalism, admits, albeit unconsciously, the truth of the Marxian materialistic conception of history. This book, however, is chiefly remarkable for its impudent and shameless misrepresentations of Marx and Marxism, but these very lies show that intelligent apologists of capitalism know that their only dangerous foe is Marxian socialism.

But just as according to the vulgar superstition the tail of a snake that has been killed wiggles till sundown, so this book of Mallock's is merely a false show of life made by a theory that received its deathblow long since. It is the wiggling of the tail of the snake that Herbert Spencer killed thirty years ago with his little book "The Study of Sociology." The environment philosophy in one form or another has come to occupy the entire field of human thought. We now look for the explanation of every phenomenon in the conditions that surrounded its birth and development. The best application of this environment philosophy to intellectual and literary phenomena that has ever been made is Taine's History of English Literature.

But while Spencer's Study of Sociology is the most signal and brilliant refutation of the Great Man theory, no one man really killed that theory. The general spread and acceptance of Darwinism has produced an intellectual atmosphere in which such a theory can no more live than a fish can live out of water.

By Darwinism we mean, as you know, the transmutation of species by variation and natural selection--selection accomplished mainly, if not solely, by the struggle for existence. Now this doctrine of organic development and change or metamorphic evolution, which was, with its originators, Wallace and Darwin, a purely biological doctrine, was transported to the field of sociology by Spencer and applied with great power to all human institutions, legal, moral, economic, religious, etc. Spencer has taught the world that all social institutions are fluid and not fixed. As Karl Marx said in the preface to the first edition of Capital: "The present society is no solid crystal, but an organization capable of change, and is constantly changing," and again in the preface to the second edition, "Every historically developed social form is in fluid movement." This is the theory of Evolution in its broadest sense, and it has struck a death-blow to the conception of Permanence so dear to the hearts of the bourgeoisie who love to sing to their Great God, Private Property, "As it was in the beginning, is now and ever shall be, world without end. Amen." "Saecula saeculorum." "For the Ages of Ages."

Before natural science had thus revolutionized the intellectual atmosphere, great men proclaiming the doctrines of modern socialism might have been rained down from Heaven, but there would have been no socialist movement. In fact many of its ideas had found utterance centuries before, but the economic conditions, and consequently the intellectual conditions were not ripe, and these ideas were still-born, or died in infancy.

The general acceptance of the idea that all things change, that property, marriage, religion, etc., are in process of evolution and are destined to take on new forms prepared the way for Socialism. A man who has read Wallace and Darwin is ready to read Marx and Engels.

Now the story of the birth of Darwinism is itself a proof of the fallacy of the Great Man theory, and a signal confirmation of the view that new ideas, theories and discoveries emanate from the material conditions. The role of the great man is still an important one. We need the men who are capable of abstract thought, capable of perceiving the essential relations and significance of the facts, and of drawing correct inductions from them. Such men are rare, but there are always enough of them to perform these functions. And the Great Man, born out of due time, before the material and economic conditions are ripe for him, can effect nothing. When the conditions are ripe, the new idea always occurs to more than one man; that is, the same conditions and facts force the same idea upon different minds. It is true there is always some one man who gives this idea its best expression or best marshals the evidence of the facts in its support, and the idea usually becomes inseparably linked with his name. In this way does our race express its gratitude to its great men and perpetuate their memory.

Darwinism or the theory of Natural Selection was in this way independently discovered by Alfred Russell Wallace and Charles Darwin, and the popular judgment has not erred in giving the chief credit to Charles Darwin.

Wallace's paper "On the Law which has Regulated the Introduction of New Species," written by Wallace on one of the far-away islands of the Malay Archipelago, where he was studying the Geographical Distribution of Species, appeared in the "Annals of Natural History" in 1855. Its resultant conclusion was "that every species has come into existence coincident both in space and time with a preexisting closely allied species." Mr. Darwin tells us that Mr. Wallace wrote him that the cause to which he attributed this coincidence was no other than "generation with modification," or in other words that the "closely allied ante-type" was the parent stock from which the new form had been derived by variation.

Mr. Wallace's second paper, which in my judgment is the clearest and best condensed statement of the Doctrine of the Struggle for Existence and the principle of Natural Selection ever written, was written by Mr. Wallace at

Ternate in the Malay Archipelago, in February, 1858, and sent to Mr. Darwin. It was called "On the Tendency of Varieties to Depart Indefinitely from the Original Type." Mr. Wallace requested Mr. Darwin to show it to Sir Chas. Lyell, the father of Modern Geology, and accordingly Dr. Hooker, the great botanist, brought it to Sir Chas. Lyell. They were both so struck with the complete agreement of the conclusions of Mr. Darwin and Mr. Wallace that they thought it would be unfair to publish one without the other, so this paper and a chapter from Darwin's unpublished manuscript of the "Origin of Species" were read before the Linnaean Society on the same evening and published in their Proceedings for 1858, and thus appeared in the same year, 1859, as Marx's Critique of Political Economy. This theory of Natural Selection is, you know, in brief, that more animals of every kind are born than can possibly survive, than can possibly get a living. This gives rise to a Battle for Life. In this battle those are the victors who are the best able to secure food for themselves and their offspring and are best able by fight or flight to protect themselves from their enemies. This is called the Law of the Survival of the Fittest, but remember, the Fittest are not always the best or most highly developed forms, but simply those forms best suited to the then existing environment. These two extremely interesting papers of Wallace are printed as the two first chapters of his book "Natural Selection and Tropical Nature," published by MacMillan, a book so fascinating I would beg all my hearers and readers who have not read it to do so.

This law of double or multiple discovery holds good of all great discoveries and inventions, and is notably true of the first of the three great thoughts that we ordinarily associate with the name of Karl Marx. These three are:

1. The Materialistic Conception of History.

2. The Law of Surplus Value.

3. The Class Struggle--the third being a necessary consequence of the first two.

Now the Materialistic Conception of History was independently discovered by Engels just as Darwinism was by Wallace, as you will see by reading Engels' preface to the Communist Manifesto. But just as Wallace gave Darwin all the credit, so Engels did to Marx.

FOOTNOTE:

[1] This essay was originally prepared for and delivered as a Lecture before the Young Mens' Socialist Literary Society, an organization of Jewish Socialists on the lower East Side of New York city, in the early part of the winter of 1899-1900.

I

THE MATERIALISTIC CONCEPTION OF HISTORY

What do we mean by the Doctrine of the Materialistic Conception of History, or of "Economic Determinism," as Ferri calls it? We must make sure we understand, for there is cant in Socialism, just as there is in religion, and there is good reason to fear many of us go on using these good mouth-filling phrases, "Materialistic Conception of History," "Class-Conscious Proletariat," "Class Struggle," and "Revolutionary Socialism," with no more accurate idea of their meaning than our pious friends have of the theological phrases they keep repeating like so many poll-parrots.

At bottom, when we talk intelligently of the Materialistic Conception of History, we simply mean, what every man by his daily conduct proves to be true, that the bread and butter question is the most important question in life. All the rest of the life of the individual is affected, yes dominated the way he earns his bread and butter. As this is true of individuals, so also it is true of societies, and this gives us the only key by which we can understand the history of the past, and, within limits, predict the course of future development.

That is all there is of it. That is easy to understand, and every man of common sense is bound to admit that that much is true.

The word "materialistic" suggests philosophy and metaphysics and brings to our minds the old disputes about monism and dualism, and the dispute between religious people who believe in the existence of spirit and scientists who adopt modern materialistic monism. But no matter what position a man may hold on these philosophical and theological questions he can with perfect consistency recognize the fact that the economic factor is the dominant, determining factor in every day human life, and the man who admits this simple truth believes in the Marxian Materialistic Conception of History. The political, legal, ethical and all human institutions have their roots in the economic soil, and any reform that does not go clear to the roots and affect the economic structure of society must necessarily be abortive. Any thing that does go to the roots and does modify the economic structure, the bread and butter side of life, will inevitably modify every other branch and department of human life, political, ethical, legal, religious, etc. This makes the social question an economic question, and all our thought and effort should be concentrated on the economic question.[2]

I am aware of the fact that in the Preface of his "Socialism, Utopian and Scientific," Engels apparently identifies the Materialistic Conception of History with Materialistic Monism in Philosophy, but this connection or identification is not a necessary logical consequence of any statement of the Materialistic Conception of History I have been able to find by Engels, Marx, Deville, Ferri, Loria, or any Marxian of authority and to thus identify it, is detrimental to the cause of Socialism, since many people who would not hesitate to admit the predominance of the economic factor, instantly revolt at the idea of Materialism.

Let us take Engels' statement of this doctrine in the preface to the Manifesto. It is as follows:

"In every historical epoch, the prevailing mode of economic production and exchange, and the social organization necessarily following from it, form the basis upon which is built up, and from which alone can be explained the political and intellectual history of that epoch."

Does not that agree exactly with the doctrine as I have stated it? Or, take this statement of it by Comrade Vail, of Jersey City:

"The laws, customs, education, public opinion and morals are controlled and shaped by economic conditions, or, in other words, by the dominant ruling class which the economic system of any given period forces to the front. The ruling ideas of each age have been the ideas of its ruling class, whether that class was the patricians of ancient Rome, the feudal barons of the middle ages, or the capitalists of modern times. The economic structure of society largely controls and shapes all social institutions, and also religious and philosophical ideas."

Or, take this, by Marx himself: "The mode of production obtaining in material life determines, generally speaking, the social, political and intellectual processes of life."

Does not that again agree exactly with the doctrine as I have stated it?

The doctrine is stated in nearly the same language by Loria and Ferri, though Ferri calls it Economic Determinism, which seems to me a much better and more exact name. Ferri points out that we must not forget the intellectual factor and the various other factors, which though they are themselves determined by the economic factor, in their turn become causes acting concurrently with the economic factor. Loria deals with this whole subject most exhaustively and interestingly in his recently translated book "The Economic Foundations of Society." Curiously enough in this long book he never once gives Marx the credit of having discovered this theory, but constantly talks as though he--Loria--had revealed it to a waiting world. The method of his book is the reverse of scientific, as he first states his theory and conclusions and then starts to scour the universe for facts to support them, instead of first collecting the facts and letting them impose the theory upon his mind. And his book is by no means free from inconsistencies and contradictions. But while you cannot place yourselves unreservedly and confidingly in his hands as you can in those of Karl Marx, still his book has much value. He shows most interestingly how all the connective institutions, as he calls religious and legal and political institutions, have been moulded in the interest of the economically dominant class, and how useful they have been in either persuading or forcing the so-called "lower classes" to submit to the economic conditions that were absolutely against their interests. But the system of Wage Slavery is such a beautifully automatic system, itself subjugating the workers and leaving them no choice, that I cannot see that the capitalists have any further need of any of these connective institutions save the State. At all events, these institutions are fast losing their power over the minds of men. But the most valuable part of his book is the immense mass of evidence he has collected showing how political sovereignty follows economic sovereignty or rather, revenue, and how all past history has been made up of a series of contests between various kinds of revenue, particularly between rent from landed property and profits from industrial or manufacturing capital, but as this is nothing more than the Class Struggle between the landed aristocracy and the bourgeoisie, a struggle sketched by master hands in the Communist Manifesto of Marx and Engels, we can give Loria no credit for originality, but merely praise his industry in collecting evidence.

Gabriel Deville, who has probably done more than any one else to popularize the ideas of Marx in France, has pointed out a very nice distinction here. Man, like all living beings, is the product of his environment. But while animals are affected only by the natural environment, man's brain, itself a product of the natural environment, becomes a cause, a creator, and makes for man an economic environment, so that man is acted on by two environments, the natural environment which has made man and the economic environment which man has made. Now in the early stages of human development, it is the natural environment, the fertility of the soil, climatic conditions, abundance of game, fish, etc., which is all-important, but with the progress of civilization, the natural environment loses in relative importance, and the economic environment (machinery, factories, improved appliances, etc.) grows in importance until in our day the economic environment has become well nigh all-important. Hence the inadequacy of the Henry George theory which places all its stress on one element of the natural environment, land, and wholly neglects the dominant economic environment.

But while this economic environment, the dominant factor in human life, is the child of the brain of man, man in its creation has been forced to work within strict limitations. He had to make it out of the materials furnished him in the first place by the natural environment and later by the natural environment and the inherited economic environment, so that in the last analysis the material and economic factors are supreme.

We Marxians are often accused of neglecting the intellectual factor and, as Deville says, a whole syndicate of factors; but we do not neglect them. We recognize their existence and their importance, but we do refuse to waste our revolutionary energy on derivative phenomena when we are able to see and recognize the decisive, dominant factor, the economic factor. As Deville says, we do not neglect the cart because we insist upon putting it behind the horse instead of in front of or alongside of him, as our critics would have us do. Now, if the economic factor is the basic factor, it behooves us to understand the present economic system--Marx's Law of Surplus-Value is the key to this system.

FOOTNOTE:

[2] If this be true the question naturally arises: Why do the socialists, instead of using economic methods to solve an economic question, organize themselves into a political party? To answer this question, we must first see what the State is and what relation it holds to the economic conditions. Gabriel Deville defines the State thus: "The State is the public power of coercion created and maintained in human societies by their division into classes, a power which, being clothed with force, makes laws and levies taxes." As long as the economically dominant class retain full possession of this public power of coercion they are able to use it as a weapon to defeat every attempt to alter

the economic structure of society. Hence every attempt to destroy economic privilege and establish Industrial Democracy inevitably takes the form of a political class struggle between the economically privileged class and the economically exploited class.

II

THE LAW OF SURPLUS-VALUE

The second great idea that we associate with the name of Karl Marx is the Law of Surplus-Value. Curiously enough this one technical theory is the only discovery that bourgeois writers and economists give Marx credit for. If you look up Marx in any ordinary encyclopedia or reference book you will find they make his fame depend on this theory alone, and to make matters worse they usually misstate and misrepresent this theory, while they invariably fail to mention his two other equally great, if not greater discoveries, the Materialistic Conception of History and the Class Struggle. I think the reason they give special prominence to this law of Surplus-Value is that, as it is a purely technical theory in economics, it is easier to obscure it with a cloud of sophistry and persuade their willing dupes that they have refuted it. And then they raise the cry that the foundation of Marxian Socialism has been destroyed and that the whole structure is about to tumble down on the heads of its crazy defenders, the Socialists. It is much to be regretted that many so-called Socialists are found foolish enough to play into the hands of the Capitalists by joining in the silly cry that some pigmy in political economy has overthrown the Marxian theory of Value. I suppose these so-called Socialists are actuated by a mad desire to be up to date, to keep up with the intellectual band-wagon. Revolutions in the various sciences have been going on so rapidly, they fancy that a theory that was formulated forty years ago must be a back-number, and so they hasten to declare their allegiance to the last new cloud of sophistry, purporting to be a theory of value, that has been evolved by the feeble minds of the anarchists of Italy or the capitalist economists of Austria. The Fabians of London are the most striking example of these socialists whose heads have been turned in this way by the rapid progress of science. But the followers of

Bernstein in Europe and this country are running into the same danger and in their eagerness to grasp the very newest and latest doctrine will fall easy victims of the first windy and pretentious fakir who comes along. Ask any one of these fellows who tells you that the Marxian theory of Value has been exploded, to state the new and correct theory of Value that has taken its place and you will find that he cannot state a theory that you or I or any other man can understand. He will either admit he is floored, or else he will emit a dense fog of words. I challenge any one of them to state a theory of value that he himself can understand, let alone make any one else understand.

Now the Marxian theory of Value can be clearly stated so that you and I can understand it. But let us begin with surplus-value. This theory of surplus-value is simply the scientific formulation of the fact that workingmen had been conscious of in a vague way long before Karl Marx's day, the fact that the workingman don't get a fair deal, that he don't get all he earns. This fact had been formulated as long ago as 1821 by the unknown author of a letter to Lord John Russell on "The Source and Remedy of the National Difficulties." In this letter the very phrases "surplus produce" and "surplus labor" are used. You will find that Marx refers to this letter in a note on page 369 (Humboldt edition, 644 Kerr edition) of the American edition of Capital. The Russian writer, Slepzoff, quotes several passages from this letter in an article in the December, 1899, number of La Revue Socialiste, and it is amazing to see how near to Marx's conclusions this unknown writer had come eighty years ago, but the conditions were not ripe and his letter would to-day be forgotten if Marx had not embalmed it in a footnote. I confess I was surprised to learn that this was not a purely original discovery of Marx's, but the fact that it is not is one more signal confirmation of the theory I have given in this lecture of the double or multiple discovery of great ideas.

But let us resume the discussion of Surplus Value and see just what it really is.

No matter where you, my workingman hearer or reader may work, the person or corporation or trust for whom or which you work gets back more out of your labor, than he or it pays you in wages. If this is not so, your employer is either running a charitable institution or he is in business for his health. You may have employers of that kind here on the East Side of New York, but I have never met any of them elsewhere. It is impossible to conceive of a man going on day after day, week after week, year after year, paying you wages, unless he receives more for the product of your labor than he pays you in wages. Now, this difference between what you get and what he gets is what we call surplus-value.

This surplus-value is the key to the whole present economic organization of society. The end and object of bourgeois society is the formation and accumulation of surplus-value, or in other words, the systematic robbery of the producing class. Now when we say robbery, we do not mean to accuse employers of conscious dishonesty. They are the creatures of a system just as the workers are, but it is a system which makes their interests diametrically opposed to the interests of their employees. The only way the capitalists can increase their relative share of the product of their employees' labor is by decreasing the relative share of the latter.

Now, if out of the total product of his labor the workingman only receives a part, then it is true to say that he works part of the day for himself and part of the day gratuitously for the capitalist. Let us say, for purposes of illustration, that he works three hours for himself and seven hours for his employer for nothing. This three hours we call his necessary labor time, or his paid labor; and the seven hours we call his surplus labor time or his unpaid labor. The product of his three hours' labor is the equivalent of his wages or as we call it, the value of his Labor-Power. The product of the other seven hours of his labor, his surplus or unpaid labor, is surplus product or surplus-value. Starting from the fact that every workingman knows to be true, that he don't get all he feels he ought to get, we have thus, I think, made the definition of surplus-value clear to every one of you, but we have been talking of surplus-value and value of labor power and we have not yet defined Value.

When we speak of the value of an object we mean the amount of human labor that is embodied or accumulated in it, that has been spent in fitting it to satisfy human needs. And we measure the amount of this human labor by its duration, by labor-time. You, if you are a skilled, highly-paid worker, receiving say four dollars a day, may say that it is absurd to say that an hour of your labor produces no more value than an hour of Tom's or Dick's or Pete's, who get only eighty cents a day apiece. You are quite right. Your hour does produce more value. The labor-time that determines value is the labor-time of the average, untrained worker. Again, you may waste your time, spending half of it looking out of the window or carrying on a flirtation. This wasted labor does not count in measuring value. The only labor that counts is the labor that is socially necessary under normal conditions for the production of the given commodity. Again, labor spent to produce a useless article does not produce value. To produce value the labor must serve to satisfy human wants. Now, I think this is quite clear so far. We know what surplus-value is. We know what value is and how it is measured. Let us now see what is meant by the Value of Labor-Power.

To begin with, what is Labor-Power? When a workingman goes upon the market to sell something for money with which to buy bread and butter and other necessaries of life, what has he to offer for sale? He cannot offer a finished commodity, such as a watch, a shoe, or a book, because he owns nothing. He has neither the necessary machinery, the necessary raw material, nor even the necessary place in which to work to make these things. These all belong to another class who by owning them, in fact, own him. He cannot offer labor for sale, because his labor does not yet exist. He cannot sell a thing that has no existence. When his labor comes into real objective existence, it is incorporated with materials that are the property of the class that rules him, and no longer belongs to him. He cannot sell what he don't possess. There is only one thing he can sell, namely, his mental and physical or muscular power to do things, to make things. He can sell this for a definite time to an employer, just exactly as a livery stable keeper sells a horse's power to trot to his customers for so much per hour. Now this power of his to do things is what we call his labor-power; that is, his capacity to perform work. Now, its value is determined precisely like the value of every other commodity, i. e., by the labor-time socially necessary for its production. Now the labor-time socially necessary for the production of labor-power is the labor-time socially necessary to produce the food, clothing and shelter or lodging that are necessary to enable the laborer to come on the labor market day after day able physically to work, and also to enable him to beget and raise children who will take his place as wage-slaves when he shall have been buried by the County or some Sick and Death Benefit Fund.

In the example we used above we assumed that the laborer worked three hours a day to produce a value equal to the value of his labor-power. The price of this value, the value produced by his paid labor, we call "Wages." This price is often reduced by the competition of "scabs" and other victims of capitalist exploitation, below the real value of labor-power, but we have not time to go into that here, so we will assume that the laborer gets in wages the full value of his labor-power.

Well, then, if he produces in three or four hours a value equal to the value of his labor-power or wages, why doesn't he stop work then, and take his coat and hat and go home and devote the rest of the day to study, reading, games, recreation and amusement? He don't because he can't. He has to agree (voluntarily, of course) to any conditions that the class who by owning his tools own him choose to impose upon him, and the lash of the competition of the unemployed, Capital's Reserve Army, as Marx called it, is ever ready to fall upon his naked back.

Why is he so helpless? Because he and his class have been robbed of the land and the tools and all the means of sustenance and production, and have nothing left them but that empty bauble, legal liberty, liberty to accept wages so small that they barely enable them to live like beasts, or liberty to starve to death and be buried in unmarked graves by the public authorities.

The wage system necessarily implies this surplus labor or unpaid labor. So long as there are wages, workingmen, you will never get the full product of your labor. Let no reformer beguile you into a struggle which simply aims to secure a modification of the wage system! Nothing short of the annihilation of the wage system will give you justice and give you the full product of your labor.

But while wages necessarily imply surplus-labor, the reverse is not true. You can have surplus-labor without wages. Surplus-labor is not an invention of modern capitalists. Since Mankind emerged from the state of Primitive Communism typified by the Garden of Eden in the Hebraic myth, there have been three great systems of economic organization: 1. Slavery; 2. Serfdom; 3. The Wage System. It is interesting to note the varying appearances of surplus or unpaid labor under these three systems.

Under the first, Slavery, all labor appears as unpaid labor. This is only a false appearance, however. During a part of the day the slave only reproduces the value of his maintenance or "keep." During that part of the day he works for himself just as truly as the modern wage slave works for himself during a part of his day. But the property relation conceals the paid labor.

Under the second system, Serfdom, or the Feudal System,--the paid labor and the unpaid labor are absolutely separate and distinct, so that not even the most gifted orthodox political economist can confuse them.

Under the third system, Wage Slavery, the unpaid labor apparently falls to Zero. There is none. You voluntarily enter into a bargain, agreeing that your day's work is worth so much, and you receive the full price agreed upon. But again this is only a false appearance. As we saw by our analysis, a part of the wage-slave's day is devoted to paid labor and a part to unpaid. Here wages or the money relation conceals the unpaid labor and disguises under the mask of a voluntary bargain the struggle of the working class to diminish or abolish unpaid labor, and the class-conscious, pitiless struggle of the capitalist class to increase the unpaid labor and reduce the paid labor to the minimum, i. e., to or below the level of bare subsistence. In other words the Wage System conceals the Class Struggle.

III

THE CLASS STRUGGLE

The third of the great ideas that will always be associated with the name of Karl Marx is that of the Class Struggle. The Class Struggle is logically such a necessary consequence of both the Materialistic Conception of History and the Law of Surplus-Value, that as we have discussed them at some length, but little need be said of the Class Struggle itself. In discussing the Materialistic Conception of History we showed with sufficient fullness and clearness that, in the language of the Communist Manifesto, "The history of all hitherto existing society is the history of Class Struggles." Hence it is clear the doctrine of class struggles is a key to past history. But it is more than this. It is a compass by which to steer in the present struggle for the emancipation of the proletariat, who cannot, fortunately, emancipate themselves without emancipating and ennobling all mankind.

The Law of Surplus-Value has shown us that there is a deep-seated, ineradicable conflict between the direct class interest of the proletariat which coincides with the true interests of the human race, and the direct, conscious guiding interest of the class who own the means of production and distribution. There is here a direct clash between two hostile interests. This fact has been skilfully hidden from the eyes of the workers in the past, but the modern socialist movement, aided by the growing brutality of the capitalist class, is making it impossible to fool them in this way much longer. In other words, the workingmen are becoming Class-Conscious, i. e., conscious of the fact that they, as a class, have interests which are in direct conflict with the selfish interests of the capitalist class. With the growth of this class-consciousness this conflict of interests must inevitably become a political class struggle. The capitalists, the economically privileged class, struggle to retain possession of the State that they may continue to use it as a weapon to keep the working class subjugated, servile and dependent. The proletariat, the working-class, struggle to obtain possession of the State, that they may use it to destroy every vestige of economic privilege, to abolish private property in the means of production and distribution, and thus put an end to the division of society into classes, and usher in the society of the future, the Co-operative Commonwealth. As the State is in its very nature a class instrument, as its existence is dependent upon the existence of distinct classes, the State in the hands of the victorious proletariat will commit suicide, by tearing down its own foundation.

Until a man perceives and is keenly conscious of this class conflict, a conflict which admits of no truce or compromise, and ranges himself on the side of the workers to remain there until the battle is fought and the victory won, until the proletariat shall have conquered the public powers, taken possession of that class instrument, the State (for so long as the State exists it will be a class instrument) and made it in the hands of the working class a tool to abolish private ownership in the tools and the land, in the means of production and distribution, and to abolish all classes by absorbing them all in the Brotherhood of Man; until a man has thus shown himself clearly conscious of the Class Struggle, with its necessary implications, his heart may be in the right place, but laboring men can not trust him as a leader. The fact that the hearts of many popular reformers, political candidates and so-called "friends of labor," who ignore the class struggle, are on the right side, but gives them added power to mislead and betray workingmen. Workingmen, I beg you to follow no leader who has not a clear enough head to see that there is a class struggle, and a large enough heart to place himself on your side of that struggle. But remember that you are not fighting the battle of a class alone. You are fighting for the future welfare of the whole human race. But while this is true, it is also true that your class must bear the brunt of this battle, for yours is the only class that, in the language of the Manifesto, "has nothing but its chains to lose, and a World to gain!" The rich have much to lose, and this very real and tangible risk of loss not unnaturally blinds the eyes of most of them to the more remote, though infinitely greater compensations that Socialism has to offer them. The Middle Class, even down to those who are just a round above the proletarians on the social ladder, love to ape the very rich and the capitalist magnates. It tickles their silly vanity to fancy that their interests are capitalistic interests, and their mental horizon is too hopelessly limited for them to perceive that the proletariat whom it pleases them to despise as the great army of the "unwashed" are in truth fighting their battles for them, and receiving instead of gratitude, contempt, gibes and sneers. Socialism does occasionally receive a recruit from the very highest stratum of society, but I tell you it is easier for a camel to pass through the eye of a needle than it is for a member of the Middle Class to become a scientific socialist.

I have said the Class Struggle is a compass to steer by in the present struggle for the emancipation of the working class. If we steer by this compass, we will resolutely reject all overtures from political parties representing the interests of other classes, even when such parties in their platform endorse some of the immediate demands of the socialists; we will "fear the Greeks bringing gifts;" we will not be seduced for a moment by the idea of fusion with any so-called Socialist party which is not avowedly based on the Class Struggle; especially as individuals will we avoid giving our votes or our support to any Middle Class party which we may at times fancy to be "moving in the right direction." The history of the class conflicts of the past shows that whenever the proletarians have joined forces with the Middle Class or any section of it, the proletarians have had to bear the heat and burden of the day and when the victory has been won their allies have robbed them of its fruits.

You, yourselves, then, Workingmen, must fight this battle! To win, it is true, you will need the help of members of the other classes. But this help the economic evolution is constantly bringing you. It is a law of the economic evolution that with the progress of industrialism the ratio of the returns of capital to the capital invested constantly diminishes, (though the aggregate volume of those returns increases). You see this in the constant lowering of the rate of interest. Now, as their incomes decrease, the small capitalists and the middle class, who form the vast majority of the possessing class, become unable to continue to support the members of the liberal professions, the priests, preachers, lawyers, editors, lecturers, etc., whose chief function heretofore has been to fool the working class into supporting or at least submitting to the present system. Now, when the income of these unproductive laborers, an income drawn from the class hostile to the proletariat, shall sensibly decrease or, worse still, cease, these educated members of the liberal professions will desert the army of Capital and bring a much-needed reinforcement to the Army of Labor.

Some of the more far-seeing upholders of the present system are keenly conscious of this danger. And this danger (even though most of the expansionists may not realize it), is one of the most potent causes of the Imperialism, Militarism, and Jingoism which are at present disgracing the civilized world. England in Africa, and America in the Philippines are pursuing their present criminal policies, not solely to open new markets for English and American goods, but also to secure new fields for the investment of English and American capital, and thus to stop the continuous dropping of the rate of interest and profits, for if this cannot be stopped, the intellectual proletariat will join the sweating proletariat, and the Co-operative Commonwealth will be established and then the poor capitalists will have to work for their livings like other people.

This was clearly pointed out by a capitalist writer in an essay in a recent number of the Atlantic Monthly, who warned the capitalist opponents of McKinley, Destiny & Co.'s policy of expansion that they were attempting to close the only safety-valve which under present conditions could, not avert, but postpone the Social Revolution.[3]

But, friends, nothing can postpone it long, for the industrial crises and financial panics are recurring at shorter and shorter intervals, and the process of recovery from them is slower and slower, and every panic and crisis forces thousands of educated, intelligent members of the middle class off their narrow and precarious foothold down into the ranks of the proletariat, where the hard logic of the facts will convert them to class-conscious Socialism.

Workingmen, I congratulate you upon the approaching victory of the workers and the advent of the Co-operative Commonwealth, for I tell you, in the language of an English comrade:

"Failure on failure may seem to defeat us; ultimate failure is impossible.

Seeing what is to be done then, seeing what the reward is,

Seeing what the terms are,--are you willing to join us? Will you lend us the aid of your voice, your money, your sympathy?

May we take you by the hand and call you 'Comrade'?"

FOOTNOTE:

[3] The expansion policy also acts as a safety-valve by promoting the emigration of the discontented and by providing employment abroad for the educated proletarians who would, no doubt, become "dangerous and incendiary Socialist agitators" in their native lands.

MARXISM AND ETHICS

(Wilshire's Magazine, November, 1905).

What are "wrong," "right," "vice," "virtue," "bad" and "good"? Mere whips to scourge the backs that naked bear The burden of the world--bent backs that dare Not rise erect, defy the tyrant, "Should," And freely, boldly do the things they would. In living's joy they rarely have a share; They look beyond the grave, and hope that there They'll be repaid, poor fools, for being good.

To serve thy master, that is virtue, Slave; To do thy will, enjoy sweet life, is vice. Poor duty-ridden serf, rebel, forget Thy master-taught morality; be brave Enough to make this earth a Paradise Whereon the Sun of Joy shall never set!

Thanks to modern science--the child of the machine process--the universality of the law of cause and effect is now assumed on all hands. In Labriola's strong words, "Nothing happens by chance." The Marxist believes this in all its fulness. To him systems of religion, codes of ethics and schools of art are, in the last analysis, just as much products of material causes as are boots or sausages. There are some intellectual Socialists whose mode of life has shielded them from the discipline of the Machine Process--the inexorable inculcator of causation--who attempt to place religion and ethics and other ideological phenomena in a separate category not to be accounted for by the materialistic conception of history. These may turn to Marx and weary their auditors by their iteration of "Lord! Lord!" but verily they know not the mind of the Master.

With Marx matter always comes first, thought second. The dialectic materialism of the Socialist is an all-inclusive philosophy, accounting for all phenomena--as fully for those called spiritual as for the most grossly material.

The man who narrows this dialectic materialism down to economic determinism and then defines the latter as meaning that the economic factor has been the "dominant" factor--among many independent factors--in producing the civilization of to-day, may be a sincere Socialist, but he is no Marxist.

The work of the theoretical Marxist will not be done till the origin and development of all religions, philosophies, and systems of ethics have been explained and accounted for by reference to material and economic causes. To understand history the primary requisite is to understand the processes by which the material means of life have been produced and distributed.

"The ruling ideas of every age have ever been the ideas of its ruling class." This applies of ideas of right and wrong--of what is commonly known as morality--as fully as to ideas of any other kind.

Conduct that has tended to perpetuate the power of the economically dominant class--since the increase of wealth has divided society into classes-- has ever been accounted moral conduct; conduct that has tended to weaken or subvert the power of the ruling class has always been branded as immoral. There you have the key to all the varying codes of ethics the world has seen.

For it must never be forgotten that ideas of right and wrong are not absolute, but relative; not fixed, but fluid, changing with the changes in our modes of producing food, clothes and shelter. Morality varies not only with time, but with social altitude. What was accounted a virtue in a bold baron of the feudal days was a crime in that same baron's serf. The pipe-line hand who regulates his daily life by the same moral ideas which have made John D. Rockefeller a shining example of piety will find himself behind prison bars.

Ethics simply register the decrees by which the ruling class stamps with approval or brands with censure human conduct solely with reference to the effect of that conduct upon the welfare of their class. This does not mean that any ruling class has ever had the wit to devise ab initio a code of ethics perfectly adapted to further their interests. Far from it. The process has seldom, if ever, been a conscious one. By a process akin to natural selection in the organic world, the ruling class learns by experience what conduct is helpful and what hurtful to it, and blesses in the one case and damns in the other. And as the ruling class has always controlled all the avenues by which ideas reach the so-called lower classes, they have heretofore been able to impose upon the subject classes just those morals which were best adapted to prolong their subjection. Even to-day in America the majority of the working class get their ideas--like their clothes--ready-made.

But there is an ever-growing portion of the working class whom the ever-increasing severity of the discipline of the machine process is teaching more and more to think solely in terms of material cause and effect. To them, just as much as to the scholar who has learned by study the relativity of ethics, current morality has ceased to appeal. It is idle to talk of the will of God, or of abstract, absolute ideas of right and wrong to the sociological scholar and the proletarian of the factory alike.

George Bernard Shaw, in the preface to "Plays, Pleasant and Unpleasant," says: "I have no respect for popular morality." A few weeks since, a workingman, who had been listening to a stereotyped sentimental harangue emitted by one of our amiable Utopian comrades, showed me the palms of his hands, which were thickly studded with callouses, and asked me, "What the hell has a fellow with a pair of mits like those to do with morality? What I want is the goods." Shaw meant just what he wrote; yet the critics will continue to treat his utterance as one of Bernard Shaw's "delightfully witty paradoxes." My friend meant just what he said; yet Salvation Armyists and other good Christians will continue to preach to him and his kind a religion and a morality which have become meaningless to them.

Organized government, with its power to make laws and levy taxes--in other words, the State--only came into existence with the division of society into classes. The State is, in its very essence, a class instrument--an agency in the hands of the ruling class to keep the masses in subjection. Hence the name, "State," cannot fitly be applied to the social organization of a society in which there are no classes, whether that society be the primitive communist group of savagery or the co-operative commonwealth of the future.

The word "capital," cannot be applied to the machinery and means of production in any and every society. They only become capital when they are used as means to exploit (rob) a subject class of workers, and when they shall cease to be so used they will cease to be capital. The word "wages," necessarily implies the extraction of surplus-value (profits) from the workers by a parasitic class; hence, that share of the social product which the workers of the future will devote to individual consumption cannot be correctly spoken of as "wages."

In the same way, morality is, in its very essence, a class institution--a set of rules of conduct enforced or inculcated for the benefit of a class. Hence, to speak of the morality of the future, when one refers to the classless society to which Socialists look forward, is the height or the depth of absurdity. In the free fellowship of the future there will be no morality. This is not saying that there will be no criteria by which conduct will be praised or deplored; it is simply saying that with the abolition of classes, morality, like the State, capital and wages, being a product of class-divisions, will cease to exist.

While the revolutionary proletariat have no respect for current morality, it is none the less true that they have in process of growth a morality of their own-- a morality that has already emerged from the embryonic stage. The proletariat are to be the active agents in bringing to pass the social revolution which is to put a period to Capitalism and usher in the new order. During this transition period and until the change is fully accomplished, they will be a distinct class with special class interests of their own. As fast as they become class-conscious they will recognize and praise as moral all conduct that tends to hasten the social revolution--the triumph of their class, and they will condemn as unhesitatingly as immoral all conduct that tends to prolong the dominance of the capitalist class. Already we can note manifestations of this new proletarian morality in that sense of class solidarity exhibited by the workers in the many acts of kindness and assistance of the employed to the unemployed, and more especially in the detestation in which the scab is held.

The revolutionary workingman, be he avowed Socialist or not, who repudiates the current or capitalist morality, does not abandon himself to unbridled license, but is straightway bound by the obligations of the adolescent proletarian morality which is enforced with ever greater vigor by the public opinion of his class as his class grows in class-consciousness.

Does the new morality condemn what the old branded as "crimes against property?" It must be confessed that the revolutionary worker has absolutely no respect for natural rights--including the right of property--as such. Hence, as the act of an individual in appropriating the goods of another is not likely either to help or to injure his class, he neither approves or condemns it on moral grounds; but knowing, as he does, that his class enemies, the capitalists, own not only "the goods," but also the courts and the police, he condemns theft by a workingman as suicidal folly.

The Marxist absolutely denies the freedom of the will.[4] Every human action is inevitable. "Nothing happens by chance." Every thing is because it cannot but be. How then can we consistently praise or blame any conduct? If one cares to make hair-splitting distinctions, it may be replied that we cannot, but none the less we can rejoice at some actions and deplore others. And the love of praise, with its obverse, the fear of blame, has ever been one of the strongest motives to human conduct. It is not necessarily the applause of the thoughtless multitude that one seeks; but in writing this paper, which I know will be misunderstood or condemned by the majority of those who read it, undoubtedly one of my motives is to win the approbation of the discerning few for whose good opinion I deeply care.

The passengers whose train has come to a standstill on a steep up-grade owing to the inefficiency of the engine, will not fail to greet with a hearty cheer the approach of a more powerful locomotive. In the same way, Socialist workingmen, though they know that no human act deserves either praise or blame, though they know, in the words of the wise old Frenchman, that "comprendre tout, c'est pardonner tout," or, better yet, that to understand all is to understand that there is nothing to pardon, will not be chary of their cheers to him who is able to advance their cause, nor of their curses upon him who betrays it. And in so doing they will not be inconsistent, but will be acting in strict accordance with that law of cause and effect which is the very fundament of all proletarian reasoning; for those cheers and curses will be potent factors in causing such conduct as will speed the social revolution.

While we have no respect for current morality, we must not fall into the error of supposing that there are no criteria by which to judge conduct, that there are, so to say, no valid distinctions between the acts of a hero and those of a blackguard. By referring to the ethic inspiring the actor we can always pronounce some conduct to be fine and other acts base. It is this power of a fine or noble action to thrill the human heart that makes the triumphs of dramatic art possible. The dramatists, like Shakespeare, whose characters accept the current moral code, appeal to a wide audience--to nearly all. But those dramatists, such as Ibsen, Shaw, Maeterlinck, and above all, Sudermann, whose heroes and heroines attempt to put into practice the ideals of to-morrow in the environment of to-day, are misunderstood and disliked by the majority, and understood and appreciated only by the few who, like themselves, have rejected the current code and adopted the criteria of to-morrow. But those of us who call Sudermann the first of living dramatists, do so on account of the extreme nobility of his heroines' conduct judged by the criteria of the future.

While there will be no morality in Socialist society; while in the perfect solidarity of a classless society there can be no conflict of individual with social interests; there will nevertheless be certain actions exceptionally fitted to increase the welfare and augment the happiness of the community, and the men and women who perform these acts will undoubtedly be rewarded by the plaudits and the love of their comrades. Indeed, we with our debased standards are incapable of conceiving how dear to them this reward will be. It is because I believe that this love of one's fellows under Socialism will be a joy far exceeding in intensity any pleasure known to us, that I look for dramatic art to reach under Socialism a perfection and influence to-day inconceivable.

The most striking phenomenon in the field of ethics to-day is the rapid growth of the new proletarian morality; and one of the principal functions of the Socialist agitator and propagandist is to facilitate and further this growth. He is the teacher of a new morality and, if one accepted Matthew Arnold's definition of religion as "morality touched with emotion," he might be called the preacher of a new religion. Let who will call this sentimentalism, it is none the less hard fact. For, after all, this new proletarian ethic is nothing else than class-consciousness under a new name. And what Socialist will deny that the chief function of the militant Socialist is to develop class-consciousness in the workers? The one hope of the world to-day is in the victory of the proletariat-- aye, it is more than a hope, it is a certainty; but this victory can only be won by a proletariat permeated with the sense of solidarity; and the workingman imbued with this sense of proletarian solidarity will be a living incarnation of the new morality.

And what is this class-consciousness which it is our business to preach in season and out of season? There is probably no term in the whole technical vocabulary of Socialism which grates so unpleasantly on the ear of the petit bourgeois who "is coming our way" as this one of "class-consciousness." To say class-consciousness is not to say class hatred; though class-consciousness ofttimes develops into class hatred and does not thereby become the less effective. The Socialist recognizes in the words of Edmund Burke that "Man acts not from metaphysical considerations, but from motives relative to his interests," and hence, he regards it as his first duty to show his fellow-workers that their economic interests are in direct conflict with those of the master-class. He does not create this conflict by pointing it out; he merely shows the working class "where they are at."

But besides pointing out this conflict of material interests, the Socialist propagandist shows the workers that it is their high destiny to accomplish a revolution far more glorious and pregnant with blessings for humanity than any of those recorded in the history of the past. This consciousness of the great part that he and his class are called to play on the world's stage is the most uplifting and ennobling influence that can enter the life of a workingman. There can be no doubt that the sentiment expressed by the words, noblesse oblige, has had an influence on the lives of the more worthy of the aristocrats. Similar in its nature is the influence here under consideration, and that this influence is not less potent is well known to every one acquainted with the men and women who form what is known as the Socialist Movement. The non-Socialist, who wishes to see the effect of this influence, has but to read even in the files of the capitalist press the accounts of the high and noble bearing of the martyrs of the Paris Commune who faced death with calm and cheerful courage, though they were buoyed up by no hope of a hereafter.

While we continue devoting our whole energies to arousing in our fellow-workers a keen and clear consciousness of the hideous class-struggle now waging in all its brutal bitterness, let us keep our courage high and our hope bright by keeping our eyes ever fixed upon the glorious future, upon the "wonderful days a-coming when all shall be better than well!"

FOOTNOTE:

[4] It will be seen that the text treats the long-debated question of the "freedom of the will" as res adjudicata. It may be that some readers will want

to know where to turn for fuller discussions of this famous question. As a full bibliography of the literature on this subject would more than fill this volume, I must content myself with telling them that a very helpful discussion of it may be found in Huxley's Life of Hume, and a clear and succinct statement of the conclusions of the modern school of psychology in Ferri's "The Positive School of Criminology." Both of these are to be had in cheap form.

INSTEAD OF A FOOTNOTE[5]

A photograph of a Fifth Avenue mansion, taken from the partition wall in the back-yard, might be a perfectly accurate picture and yet give a very inadequate idea of the house as a whole. This article on "Marxism and Ethics" is, in a sense, just such a picture. In writing it, space limitations compelled me to confine myself wholly to impressing upon the reader the relative and transitory character of moral codes. But in the popular concept of morality there are elements that are relatively permanent. Darwin in his "Descent of Man" showed that the gregarious and social traits that make associated life possible antedate, not only the division of society into classes, but even antedate humanity itself, since they plainly appear in the so-called lower animals.

So that my contention that morality only came into being with the division of society into classes and will pass away when class divisions are abolished, becomes a question of definition. If we include in our definition of morality the almost universal and relatively permanent gregarious traits of men and beasts, then morality has existed longer than humanity itself, and will continue to exist under Socialism. But it cannot be denied that moral codes were not formulated until after class-divisions had arisen. Every moral code of which we have any knowledge has been moulded by the cultural discipline of a society based on class-divisions. In every one of them there is implied the relation of status, of a superior, natural or supernatural, with the right or power to formulate "commandments," and of an inferior class whose lot it is to obey. We find this implication of status in even the noblest expressions of current ethical aspirations. Wordsworth's immortal Ode to Duty begins, "Stern Daughter of the Voice of God!"

Since then morality as a word through the force of immemorial habit unavoidably suggests to the mind the relation of status, it appears to me that its use to describe truly social conduct in a society of equals can lead to nothing but confusion. What we really need is the right word to apply to the highest conduct in a classless society; and, I am inclined to think that a generation to whom the idea of status will have become wholly alien will find the word "social" entirely adequate for this purpose, though I frankly confess it is not adequate for us

"In the days of the years we dwell in, that wear our lives away."

My statement that the Revolutionary worker abstains from crimes against property from expediency rather than from principle must not be construed into an allegation that fear of personal punishment is the only ground for abstaining from such crimes. If it were not for the stupidity and malice of our opponents I would feel that I was insulting my readers by making this explanation; but for their benefit be it said that in a society based economically upon the institution of private property social life is impossible without respect (respect here refers to acts, not to mental attitude) for private property. Crimes against property are distinctly unsocial. But respect for the rights of property is rapidly disintegrating both among trust magnates and proletarians. The Natural Rights Philosophy[6] still has much vitality in the middle classes, but as a broad statement it will hold good that the millionaire or the proletarian who shows respect for private property (the private property of others, be it understood) does so chiefly on grounds of expediency.

The socialist materialist is well content to leave this whole question of ethics to adjust itself, since he knows that equality of condition, the economic basis of Socialism, will necessarily evolve a mode of living, and standards of conduct in perfect harmony with their economic environment.

FOOTNOTES:

[5] It may be as well to state that this was written before the writer had read Karl Kautsky's illuminating work, "Ethics and the Materialist Conception of History."

[6] For a fuller discussion of the relation of current conceptions of property-rights to the Natural Rights Philosophy see Veblen's "The Theory of Business Enterprise," Chapters II and VIII, and La Monte's paper "Veblen, The Revolutionist," International Socialist Review, Vol. V. pp. 726-739.

THE NIHILISM OF SOCIALISM.

"In their negative proposals the socialists and anarchists are fairly agreed. It is in the metaphysical postulates of their protest and in their constructive aims that they part company. Of the two, the socialists are more widely out of touch with the established order. They are also more hopelessly negative and destructive in their ideals, as seen from the standpoint of the established order." THORSTEIN VEBLEN in "The Theory of Business Enterprise." Page 338.

To label a truth a truism is too often regarded as equivalent to placing it in the category of the negligible. It is precisely the salient obviousness, which makes a truth a truism, that places it in the direst peril of oblivion in the stress of modern life. Such a truth was well stated by Enrico Ferri, the Italian criminologist, in a recent lecture before the students of the University of Naples:

"Without an ideal, neither an individual nor a collectivity can live, without it humanity is dead or dying. For it is the fire of an ideal which renders the life of each one of us possible, useful and fertile. And only by its help can each one of us, in the longer or shorter course of his or her existence, leave behind traces for the benefit of fellow-beings."

Platitude though this may be, our greatest poets have not hesitated to use their highest powers to impress it upon us. Robert Browning put this truth into the mouth of Andrea del Sarto in one of the strongest lines in all English verse,

"Ah, but a man's reach should exceed his grasp."

Mr. George S. Street, in a very interesting paper in Putnam's Monthly for November (1906), points out that the most significant contrast between our time and Early Victorian days is a decrease in idealism. "The most characteristic note," he tells us, "in the mental attitude of the forties and fifties in England, and that in which they contrast most sharply with our own times, was confidence.... In party politics this confidence was almost without limit. There was a section of Conservatism which really believed in things as they were, and thought it undesirable to attempt any change for the better.... It was simply--I speak of a section, not the party as a whole--the articulate emotion of privileged and contented people and their parasites, and its denomination as 'stupid' was an accurate description, though hardly the brilliant epigram for which, in our poverty of political wit, it has been taken. On the other hand, there was a confident Liberalism which inspired a whole party. Some wished to go faster, some slower, but all believed sincerely in a broad scheme of domestic policy. They were to reform this and that at home; they were to assist, or at least applaud, the reforming of this and that abroad. So believing and intending, they naturally conceived themselves made very little indeed lower than the angels.

"The contrast with our own day hardly needs pointing. You might now search long and in vain for a Conservative in public life who would not admit that reforms are desirable or even urgent, though few might be prepared with precise statements about particulars.... But their (the Liberals') confidence in reform, in their ability to improve the body politic by certain definite measures, is gone. The old Liberal spirit animating a whole party is dead. It may seem an odd remark to make just after the late election, but the evidence is abundant, and the explanation simple. Domestic reform on a large scale and on individualist lines has reached its limit; but to many Liberals, to many eminent and authoritative Liberals, reform on socialist lines is abhorrent.... Consequently there is a large party called Liberal, which, through the faults of its opponents and the accidents of time, is successful and has the high spirits of success, but is no more now than it has been for twenty years a party of homogeneous confidence in domestic reform, while on the world outside the British islands it looks with passivity, perhaps timidity, certainly with no intention of assisting oppressed peoples."

* * * * *

"Theoretical Socialism of a logical and thoughtful kind, not entangled with Radicalism, has made much progress of late years, more especially, so far as my own experience goes, in the educated and professional classes; but in practice it bides its time, with confidence perhaps, but with a consciousness that the time will be long coming. That is a different spirit from the buoyant expectancy of the old Liberalism."

Granted the necessity of idealism to individual and social health, Mr. Street's views do not conduce to optimism. Here we have a competent observer telling us that the only note of idealism he finds in contemporary intellectual life is a growing, but half-hearted, belief in Socialism, which is more noticeable "in the educated and professional classes."

There is another note of idealism in the life of to-day which Mr. Street ignores. This is the tendency toward the apotheosis of the individual in antithesis to society. This is a sign of health, in so far as it is a revolt against the stifling pressure of outworn conventionality, and it has found worthy expression in the philosophy of Herbert Spencer and the poetry of Browning and Walt Whitman.

But this form of idealism cannot be said to differentiate our time from the Early Victorian era, for it found its classic expression back in the middle of the last century in Max Stirner's Der Einzige und sein Eigentum, a book which has been forgotten amid the growing consciousness of the organic solidarity of society. But Mr. Street is possibly justified in ignoring this tendency, for as a school of thought it has committed suicide in the person of Nietzsche's

Overman attempting to construct out of materials drawn from his inner consciousness a pair of stilts on which to tower above "the herd."

What is the lure of Socialism that is appealing, according to Mr. Street, to more and more of our "educated and professional" people? For, in spite of what Professor Veblen truly says of the "negative and destructive" (in the quotation at the head of this paper) character of socialist ideals, Socialism must hold up some positive ideals to attract such growing numbers of the educated classes. To convince oneself of the actuality of this appeal it is only necessary to run over the writers' names in the tables of contents in our popular magazines. The proportion of socialists is surprisingly large and is constantly growing. There can be no doubt that the percentage of Socialists among writers of distinction is larger than the percentage of socialists in the population at large.

Socialism does present certain very definite positive ideals. The first of these is "Comfort for All" (to use a chapter-heading from Prince Kropotkin's too little known book, "La Conqu 陰 e du Pain"). The second is Leisure for All, or, in Paul Lafargue's witty phrase, "The Right to be Lazy." The third is the fullest possible physical and intellectual development of every individual, considered not as an isolated, self-centred entity, but as a member of an interdependent society; or, in the words of Karl Marx and Friedrich Engels in the Communist Manifesto, the socialist ideal is "an association in which the free development of each is the condition for the free development of all."

It may be noted that all that is vivifying in the ideal of individualism is included in this third positive ideal of Socialism, so that, it is now seen, Mr. Street was fully justified in making no separate mention of the ideal of individualism. There can be no doubt that it is the immensely richer literary and artistic life promised by this third ideal of Socialism that accounts for the phenomenon noted by Mr. Street.

The beauties of the positive ideals of the socialist Utopias have been sufficiently lauded by scores of writers from Sir Thomas More to Bellamy and

Mr. H. G. Wells. What it is desired to emphasize here is the "negative and destructive" (from the standpoint of the established order) aspects of socialist ideals; for it is the Nihilism of Socialism that explains why Mr. Street's "educated and professional" socialists have more patience than confidence in awaiting the realization of their ideal. The Nihilism of Socialism turns aside many, who have felt the lure of the socialist ideal, into what Professor Veblen calls, "some excursion into pragmatic romance,"[7] such as Social Settlements, Prohibition, Clean Politics, Single Tax, Arts and Crafts, Neighborhood Guilds, Institutional Church, Christian Science, New Thought, Hearstism, or "some such cultural thimble-rig." Yet more, there are many of the "educated and professional classes" who call themselves socialists, because they cherish the charming delusion that it is possible to separate the positive from the negative ideals of Socialism, and to work (in a dilettante fashion) for the former while blithely anathematizing the latter.

It is the purpose of this paper to show that Socialism is not a scheme for the betterment of humanity to be accomplished by a sufficiently zealous and intelligent propaganda, but that it is, on the contrary, a consistent, (though to many repellent) monistic philosophy of the cosmos; that it is from its Alpha to its Omega so closely and inextricably interlocked that its component parts cannot be disassociated, save by an act of intellectual suicide; that, in a word, the Nihilism[8] of Socialism is of the very essence of Socialism.

But, here, a most important distinction should be noted. Socialism, viewed as a political propaganda, is purely positive in its demands. In fact, all its demands may be reduced to two--Collectivism and Democracy. That the people shall own the means of production, and the producers shall control their products--that is the sum and substance of all Socialist platforms. Socialist parties do not attack Religion, the Family, or the State. But socialist philosophy proves conclusively that the realization of the positive political and economic ideals of Socialism involves the atrophy of Religion, the metamorphosis of the Family, and the suicide of the State.

The Nihilism of Socialism springs from the Materialist Conception of History, and this is precisely the portion of the socialist doctrine that is usually ignored or half-understood by the enthusiastic young intellectuals who are in growing numbers joining the Socialist movement on both sides of the Atlantic. While the Communist Manifesto, written by Karl Marx and Friedrich Engels in 1847, is throughout founded on this conception, the first clearly formulated statement of the conception itself is to be found in the Preface to the "Contribution to the Critique of Political Economy," published by Karl Marx in 1859, the same year in which Darwin and Wallace made public their independent and almost simultaneous discoveries of the theory of Natural Selection. This first statement runs thus:

"In the social production which men carry on they enter into definite relations that are indispensable and independent of their will; these relations of production correspond to a definite stage of development of their material powers of production. The sum total of these relations of production constitutes the economic structure of society--the real foundation, on which rise legal and political superstructures and to which correspond definite forms of social consciousness. The mode of production in material life determines the general character of the social, political, and spiritual processes of life. It is not the consciousness of men that determines their existence, but, on the contrary, their social existence determines their consciousness. At a certain stage of their development, the material forces of production in society come in conflict with the existing relations of production, or--what is but a legal expression for the same thing--with the property relations within which they had been at work before. From forms of development of the forces of production these relations turn into their fetters. Then comes the period of social revolution. With the change of the economic foundation the entire immense superstructure is more or less rapidly transformed."[9]

This statement contains a whole Revolution in embryo. Viewed from the standpoint of the established order, it is the very Quintessence of Nihilism. In a word, it teaches the material origin of Ideas. In the last analysis, every idea can be traced back to the economic and telluric environments. In the words of Joseph Dietzgen, "philosophy revealed to them (Marx and Engels) the basic principle that, in the last resort, the world is not governed by Ideas, but, on the contrary, the Ideas by the material world." This doctrine involves a new epistemology, the distinguishing mark of which is its denial of the immaculate conception of thought. The human mind, according to Marx and Dietzgen, can only bring forth thought after it has been impregnated by the objects of sense perception.[10]

Here we have a thorough-going system of materialist monism. "Ours is the organic conception of history," says Labriola. "The totality of the unity of social life is the subject matter present to our minds. It is economics itself which dissolves in the course of one process, to reappear in as many morphological stages, in each of which it serves as a substructure for all the rest. Finally, it is not our method to extend the so-called economic factor isolated in an abstract fashion over all the rest, as our adversaries imagine, but it is, before everything else, to form an historic conception of economics, and to explain the other changes by means of its changes."[11]

In another place he says: "Ideas do not fall from heaven, and nothing comes to us in a dream.... The change in ideas, even to the creation of new methods of conception, has reflected little by little the experience of a new life. This, in the revolutions of the last two centuries, was little by little despoiled of the mythical, religious and mystical envelopes in proportion as it acquired the practical and precise consciousness of its immediate and direct conditions. Human thought, also, which sums up this life and theorizes upon it, has little by little been plundered of its theological and metaphysical hypotheses to take refuge finally in this prosaic assertion: in the interpretation of history we must limit ourselves to the objective co-ordination of the determining conditions and of the determined effects." He reiterates: "Ideas do not fall from heaven; and, what is more, like the other products of human activity, they are formed in given circumstances, in the precise fulness of time, through the action of definite needs, thanks to the repeated attempts at their satisfaction, and by the discovery of such and such other means of proof which are, as it were, the instruments of their production and their elaboration. Even ideas involve a basis of social conditions; they have their technique; thought also is a form of work. To rob the one and the other, ideas and thought, of the conditions and environment of their birth and their development, is to disfigure their nature and their meaning."[12]

This socialist materialism does not refuse the inspiration of ideals. "By granting that society is dominated by material interests," Dietzgen explains, "we do not deny the power of the ideals of the heart, mind, science, and art. For we have no more to deal with the absolute antithesis between idealism and materialism, but with their higher synthesis which has been found in the knowledge that the ideal depends on the material, that divine justice and liberty depend on the production and distribution of earthly goods."[13]

Religions, schools of ethics, philosophy, metaphysics, art, political and juridical institutions are all to be explained in the last analysis by the economic and telluric environments, present and past. This ruthless materialism crushes belief in God, in the Soul, in immortality. It leaves no room for any shred of dualism in thought. It is true that the German Social Democracy included in the famous Erfurt Programme (adopted in 1891--the first clearly Marxian socialist platform ever promulgated) a demand for a "Declaration that religion is a private matter. Abolition of all expenditure from public funds upon ecclesiastical and religious objects. Ecclesiastical and religious bodies are to be regarded as private associations, which order their affairs independently." It will be seen that this is nothing more than a demand that the State withdraw its sanction of religion as France has recently done in the Clemenceau law. But Ferri does nothing but draw the necessary conclusions from socialist premises when he writes: "God, as Laplace has said, is an hypothesis of which exact science has no need; he is, according to Herzen, at the most an X, which represents not the unknowable--as Spencer and Dubois Raymond contend--but all that which humanity does not yet know. Therefore, it is a variable X which decreases in direct ratio to the progress of the discoveries of science.

"It is for this reason that science and religion are in inverse ratio to each other; the one diminishes and grows weaker in the same proportion that the other increases and grows stronger in its struggle against the unknown."[14]

Joseph Dietzgen has thus stated what may be called the law of the atrophy of religion: "The more the idea of God recedes into the past the more palpable it is; in olden times man knew everything about his God; the more modern the form of religion has become, the more confused and hazy are our religious ideas. The truth is that the historic development of religion tends to its gradual dissolution."[15]

The characteristic attitude of the socialist materialist toward Christianity appears very clearly in the following excerpt from Professor Ferri's "Socialism and Modern Science":

"It is true that Marxian Socialism, since the Congress held at Erfurt (1891), has rightly declared that religious beliefs are private affairs[16] and that, therefore, the Socialist party combats religious intolerance under all its forms.... But this breadth of superiority of view is, at bottom, only a consequence of the confidence in final victory.

"It is because Socialism knows and foresees that religious beliefs, whether one regards them, with Sergi, as pathological phenomena of human psychology, or as useless phenomena of moral incrustation, are destined to perish by atrophy with the extension of even elementary scientific culture. This is why Socialism does not feel the necessity of waging a special warfare against these religious beliefs which are destined to disappear. It has assumed this attitude, although it knows that the absence or the impairment of the belief in God is one of the most powerful factors for its extension, because the priests of all religions have been, throughout all the phases of history, the most potent allies of the ruling classes in keeping the masses pliant and submissive under the yoke by means of the enchantment of religion, just as the tamer keeps wild beasts submissive by the terrors of the cracks of his whip" (page 63).

It is also well to remember that a prevalent animistic habit of thought in viewing the events of life, whether it take the form of a belief in luck, as in gamblers and sporting men, or the form of a belief in supernatural interposition in mundane affairs, as in the case of the devotees of the anthropomorphic cults, or merely the tendency to give a teleological interpretation to evolution, to attribute a meliorative trend to the cosmic process, as in Tennyson's "through the ages one increasing purpose runs," tends, by retarding the prompt perception of relations of material cause and effect, to lower the industrial efficiency of the community.[17]

The socialist materialist can look forward with unruffled serenity to the passing of religion, since his very definition of religion as "a popular striving after the illusory happiness that corresponds with a social condition which needs such an illusion,"[18] implies that it cannot pass away till it has ceased to be needful to human happiness.

From the point of view of this Socialist materialism, the monogamous family, the present economic unit of society, ceases to be a divine institution, and becomes the historical product of certain definite economic conditions. It is the form of the family peculiar to a society based on private property in the means of production, and the production of commodities for sale. It is not crystallized and permanent, but, like all other institutions, fluid and subject to change. With the change in its economic basis, the code of sexual morality and the monogamous family are sure to be modified; but, in the judgment of such socialists as Friedrich Engels and August Bebel, we shall probably remain monogamous, but monogamy will cease to be compulsorily permanent.[19]

"What we may anticipate," says Engels, "about the adjustment of sexual relations after the impending downfall of capitalist production is mainly of a negative nature and mostly confined to elements that will disappear. But what will be added? That will be decided after a new generation has come to maturity: a race of men who never in their lives have had any occasion for buying with money or other economic means of power the surrender of a woman; a race of women who have never had any occasion for surrendering to any man for any other reason but love, or for refusing to surrender to their lover from fear of economic consequences. Once such people are in the world, they will not give a moment's thought to what we to-day believe should be their course. They will follow their own practice and fashion their own public opinion--only this and nothing more."[20]

Changed economic conditions are already reflected in the disintegration of the traditional bourgeois belief in the permanency of the existing forms of the family and the home. A portentous sign of the times for the conservatives is the appearance of Mrs. Elsie Clews Parsons' book on "The Family," the most scholarly work on the subject by a bourgeois writer that has yet appeared. Like all bourgeois writers Mrs. Parsons has been very chary of using materials furnished by Socialist scholars. Very striking is the absence from her very extensive bibliographical notes of the names of Marx, Engels, Bebel and Ferri. But she was compelled to avail herself freely of the wealth of materials provided by the scholarly and industrious researches of Morgan, Kautsky, and Cunow.

In her now famous Fifteenth Lecture on "Ethical Considerations," she suggests various modes of ameliorating the condition of Woman, and improving conjugal and family relations; but she is again and again driven to admit that the economic independence of women is a condition precedent to her "reforms." Most of her suggestions are tinged with the utopian fancifulness characteristic of the bourgeois theorist. Two excerpts will illustrate these points sufficiently:

"Again reciprocity of conjugal rights and duties is desirable for parenthood. If marriage have a proprietary character, neither the owner nor the owned is entirely fit to develop free personalities in his or her children. Moreover the idea of marital ownership more or less involves that of parental ownership, and the latter, as we have seen, is incompatible with a high type of parenthood. The custom of proprietary marriage inevitably leads, for example, to restrictions upon female education. Now just in so far as a woman's education is limited is she handicapped as an educator of her children. It is unfortunate that in the emancipation of woman agitation of the past half-century the reformers failed to emphasize the social as adequately as the individualistic need of change. If women are to be fit wives and mothers they must have all, perhaps more, of the opportunities for personal development that men have. All the activities hitherto reserved to men must at least be open to them, and many of these activities, certain functions of citizenship[21] for example, must be expected of them. Moreover, whatever the lines may be along which the fitness of women to labor will be experimentally determined, the underlying position must be established that for the sake of individual and race character she is to be a producer as well as a consumer of social values.[22] As soon as this ethical necessity is generally recognized the conditions of modern industry will become much better adapted to the needs of women workers than they are now, the hygiene of workshop, factory, and office will improve, and child bearing and rearing will no longer seem incompatible with productive activity" (pages 345-347).

Here follows the paragraph upon which the Reverend Doctor Morgan Dix and other clerical defenders of the economic conditions that cause marital and non-marital prostitution pounced with such avidity:

"We have therefore, given late marriage and the passing of prostitution,[23] two alternatives, the requiring of absolute chastity of both sexes until marriage or the toleration of freedom of sexual intercourse on the part of the unmarried of both sexes before marriage, i. e., before the birth of offspring. In this event condemnation of sex license would have a different emphasis from that at present. Sexual intercourse would not be of itself disparaged or condemned, it would be disapproved of only if indulged in at the expense of health or of emotional or intellectual activities in oneself or in others. As a matter of fact, truly monogamous relations seem to be those most conducive to emotional or intellectual development and to health, so that, quite apart from the question of prostitution, promiscuity is not desirable or even tolerable. It would therefore, seem well from this point of view, to encourage early trial marriage,[24] the relation to be entered into with a view to permanency, but with the privilege of breaking it if proved unsuccessful and in the absence of offspring without suffering any great degree of public condemnation.

"The conditions to be considered in any attempt to answer the question that thus arises are exceedingly complex. Much depends upon the outcome of present experiments in economic independence for women, a matter which is in turn dependent upon the outcome of the general labor 'question.' Much depends upon revelations of physiological science. If the future brings about the full economic independence of women, if physiologists will undertake to guarantee society certain immunities from the sexual excess of the individual,[25] if, and these are the most important conditions of all, increases in biological, psychological and social knowledge make parenthood a more enlightened and purposive function than is even dreamed of at present and if pari passu with this increase of knowledge a higher standard of parental duty and a greater capacity for parental devotion develop, then the need of sexual restraint as we understand it may disappear and different relations between the sexes before marriage and to a certain extent within marriage may be expected."

The Socialist materialist leaves idle speculations of this nature to the bourgeois Utopians; he knows that a revolution in economic conditions must precede any material changes in sexual relations, and that when such changes take place they will take place in response to the stimuli of the transformed economic environment, and not in accordance with any preconceived notions of Mrs. Parsons or others.

Those, who are horrified at such proposed modifications of marriage as Mr. George Meredith's marriages for a fixed, limited period, and Mrs. Parsons' "trial marriages," will do well to ponder this posthumous aphorism of the clearsighted Norse genius, Ibsen, recently published in Berlin:

"To talk of 'men born free' is a mere phrase. There are none such. Marriages, the relations of man and woman, have ruined the whole race and set on all the brand of slavery."[26]

In the same case is what we may call the stage-setting of the monogamous family, the home. The home ceases to be regarded as the sacred and eternal Palladium of society. It, too, is destined to change, if not to disappear. "With the transformation of the means of production into collective property," Engels writes, "the private household changes to a social industry. The care and education of children becomes a public matter."[27]

This does not deny the splendid role that the Home has played in the history of the last three centuries. Many an English and American home to-day still merits even such an offensively pretentious epithet as "Palladium." What morals our people have known and practised they have learned and been drilled in in the homes. That these morals should have been warped by a class-bias was inevitable. A home, itself the product of a society divided into classes, could not teach anything but a class-morality. A purely social morality (if morality be the proper name for the highest conduct in a classless society) is even yet impossible.

But, much as we owe to the home, (I pity the reader who can recall his or her early home life with dry eyes), the Nihilism of Socialism tells us the day of the home is drawing to its close. So it may be as well for us to consider for a moment the bad side of the home as we know it to-day. It may be that when we have done so, we shall be able to anticipate its passing with greater equanimity.

At this late day--when seventeen years have rolled by since Ibsen's "The Doll's House" was first introduced to an English-speaking audience at the Novelty Theatre in London--it is surely not necessary to dwell upon the dwarfing and stifling effects upon women of even "happy" homes. In the brilliant preface to "Plays: Pleasant and Unpleasant," Bernard Shaw, referring to middle-class home life, speaks of "the normal English way being to sit in separate families in separate rooms in separate houses, each person silently occupied with a book, a paper, or a game of halma, cut off equally from the blessings of society and solitude." "The result," he continues, "is that you may make the acquaintance of a thousand streets of middle-class English families without coming on a trace of any consciousness of citizenship, or any artistic cultivation of the senses."

In the following paragraph he adds:

"In proportion as this horrible domestic institution is broken up by the active social circulation of the upper classes in their own orbit, or its stagnant isolation made impossible by the overcrowding of the working classes, manners improve enormously. In the middle classes themselves the revolt of a single clever daughter (nobody has yet done justice to the modern clever Englishwoman's loathing of the very word 'home'), and her insistence on qualifying herself for an independent working life, humanizes her whole family in an astonishingly short time; and the formation of a habit of going to the suburban theatre once a week, or to the Monday Popular Concerts, or both, very perceptibly ameliorates its manners. But none of these breaches in the Englishman's castle-house can be made without a cannonade of books and pianoforte music. The books and music cannot be kept out, because they alone can make the hideous boredom of the hearth bearable. If its victims may not live real lives, they may at least read about imaginary ones, and perhaps learn from them to doubt whether a class that not only submits to home life, but actually values itself on it, is really a class worth belonging to. For the sake of the unhappy prisoners of the home, then, let my plays be printed as well as acted."

A concrete picture may give us a better idea of what Shaw means when he calls women "the unhappy prisoners of the home." In that magnificent scene in the third act of "Candida," after Morell has called on Candida to choose between him and the poet, Marchbanks, Candida gives us a vivid glimpse of what her home life had been, in this speech, addressed to Marchbanks, and, in reading it, remember that Morell was "a good husband" and that Candida loved him.

"--You know how strong he (Morell) is--how clever he is--how happy! Ask James's mother and his three sisters what it cost to save James the trouble of doing anything but be strong and clever and happy. Ask me what it costs to be James's mother and three sisters and wife and mother to his children all in one. Ask Prossy and Maria how troublesome the house is even when we have no visitors to help us slice the onions. Ask the tradesmen who want to worry James and spoil his beautiful sermons who it is that puts them off. When there is money to give, he gives it: when there is money to refuse, I refuse it. I build a castle of comfort and indulgence and love for him, and stand sentinel always to keep little vulgar cares out. I make him master here, though he does not know it, and could not tell you a moment ago how it came to be so."

This should make it easy for us to understand why so many women are ready to sympathize with William Morris in the sentiments he expressed in the following paragraph in "Signs of Change:"

"As to what extent it may be necessary or desirable for people under social order to live in common, we may differ pretty much according to our tendencies toward social life. For my part I can't see why we should think it a hardship to eat with the people we work with; I am sure that as to many things, such as valuable books, pictures, and splendor of surroundings, we shall find it better to club our means together; and I must say that often when I have been sickened by the stupidity of the mean, idiotic rabbit warrens that rich men build for themselves in Bayswater and elsewhere, I console myself with visions of the noble communal hall of the future, unsparing of materials, generous in worthy ornament, alive with the noblest thoughts of our time, and the past, embodied in the best art which a free and manly people could produce; such an abode of man as no private enterprise could come anywhere near for beauty and fitness, because only collective thought and collective life could cherish the aspirations which would give birth to its beauty, or have the skill and leisure to carry them out. I for my part should think it much the reverse of a hardship if I had to read my books and meet my friends in such a place; nor do I think I am better off to live in a vulgar stuccoed house crowded with upholstery that I despise, in all respects degrading to the mind and enervating to the body to live in, simply because I call it my own, or my house."

From the viewpoint of this historical materialism, the State loses its attribute of permanence and becomes the product of definite economic conditions--in a word, it is the child of economic inequality. "The State," in the words of Engels, "is the result of the desire to keep down class conflicts. But, having arisen amid these conflicts, it is as a rule the State of the most powerful economic class that by force of its economic supremacy becomes also the ruling political class, and thus acquires new means of subduing and exploiting the oppressed masses. The antique State was, therefore, the State of the slave owners for the purpose of holding the slaves in check. The feudal State was the organ of the nobility for the oppression of the serfs and dependent farmers. The modern representative State is the tool of the capitalist exploiters of wage labor."[28]

"The State, then," Engels says on another page of the same work, "did not exist from all eternity. There have been societies without it, that had no idea of any State or public power.[29] At a certain stage of economic development, which was of necessity accompanied by a division of society into classes, the State became the inevitable result of this division. We are now rapidly approaching a stage of evolution in production, in which the existence of classes has not only ceased to be a necessity, but becomes a positive fetter on production. Hence, these classes must fall as inevitably as they once arose. The State must irrevocably fall with them. The society that is to reorganize production on the basis of a free and equal association of the producers, will transfer the machinery of the State where it will then belong--into the Museum of Antiquities by the side of the spinning wheel and the bronze ax."[30]

In another work, he says: "The first act by virtue of which the State really constitutes itself the representative of the whole of society--the taking possession of the means of production in the name of Society--this is, at the same time, its last independent act as a State. State interference in social relations becomes, in one domain after another, superfluous, and then dies out of itself; the government of persons is replaced by the administration of things, and by the conduct of processes of production. The State is not abolished. It dies out."[31]

It is thus seen that, according to the teaching of historical materialism, the

State is destined, when it becomes the State of the working-class, to remove its own foundation--economic inequality--and thus, to commit suicide.

Many of those, who have witnessed with mingled consternation and amusement the strenuous efforts of Mr. Roosevelt and the frantic zeal of Mr. Hearst to enlarge the scope of governmental action to cover every conceivable field of human activity from spelling to beef-canning, will hail with delight Engels' tidings that the State is to "die out."

The thesis, that the realization of the socialist ideal involves the atrophy of Religion, the metamorphosis of the Family, and the suicide of the State, would now appear to be sufficiently demonstrated.

One cannot help wondering what proportion of the "educated and professional" persons, who, Mr. Street testifies, are in growing numbers yielding to the lure of Socialism, really desire these results. Many of them, no doubt, are trying on a new field the old experiment of serving God and Mammon, of putting new wine into old bottles. Ibsen's Nora, though she had far less learning than is usual in the "educated and professional classes" of England and America, was, in this matter, far wiser than are they. When the falsehood and slavery of life in "The Doll's House" became unbearable to her, she knew that she must choose between the Old and the New; and that, if she chose the new life of revolt and freedom, she must leave behind her all the badges of her doll's life. Had she taken with her the trinkets and gauds that the master of the Doll's House had given her, she would not have escaped from the doll's life when she turned her back on the Doll's House. Her woman's instinct did not fail her, and, when, with a woman's courage she chose the New and left the Old, she told Torvald, "Whatever belongs to me I shall take with me. I will have nothing from you either now or later on."

Many of the young people of education, who have of late come into the socialist movement, have left--temporarily, at least--the Doll's House of conservatism; but they have brought with them many of the habits of thought, many of the conventions of their old doll's life. Some of them, doubtless, realizing that the Materialist Conception of History involves the Nihilism of Socialism, and thus calls on them to abandon their religious, metaphysical, and dualistic habits of thought, to cast aside their conventional class morality, to cease vaporing about that impossible monstrosity, "the Socialist State," attempt to cut the Gordian knot by denying the Materialist Conception of History, while clinging to their socialist ideal. They thus repeat in inverted form the curious feat in intellectual acrobatics performed by Professor Seligman, who believes in historical materialism, but rejects Socialism. "There is nothing in common," he asserts, "between the economic interpretation of history and the doctrine of socialism, except the accidental fact that the originator of both theories happened to be the same man." And a few pages further on he reiterates: "Socialism and 'historical materialism' are entirely independent-conceptions."[32]

To the educated socialists, who deny or mutilate the doctrine of historical materialism, the materialist socialist might well reply by asserting that these educated socialists are socialists only because of the artistic, intellectual, ethical, and spiritual changes they expect the economic revolution of socialism to produce. The fact that they, lovers of "the things of the spirit," are socialists proves that they believe, albeit unconsciously, in economic determinism.

But, although this personal argument might Well be deemed sufficient, it can readily be proven affirmatively that the whole theory of Modern Socialism rests upon the foundation of historical materialism. This clearly appears in the' admirable summary of the teachings of Marx that Gabriel Deville gives in the Preface to his epitome of Marx's "Capital."

"History, Marx has shown, is nothing but the history of class conflicts. The division of society into classes, which made its appearance with the social life of man, rests on economic relations--maintained by force--which enable some to succeed in shifting on to the shoulders of others the natural necessity of labor.

"Material interests have always been the inciting motives of the incessant struggles of the privileged classes, either with, each other, or against the inferior classes at whose expense they live. Man is dominated by the material conditions of life, and these conditions, and therefore the mode of production, have determined and will determine human customs, ethics, and institutions-- social, economic, political, juridical, etc.

"As soon as one part of society has monopolized the means of production, the other part, upon whom the burden of labor falls, is obliged to add to the labor-time necessary for its own support, a certain surplus-labor-time, for which it receives no equivalent,--time that is devoted to supporting and enriching the possessors of the means of production. As an extractor of unpaid labor, which, by means of the increasing surplus-value whose source it is, accumulates every day, more and more, in the hands of the proprietary class the instruments of its dominion, the capitalist regime surpasses in power all the antecedent regimes founded on compulsory labor.

"But to-day, the economic conditions begotten by this regime, trammelled in their natural evolution by this very regime, inexorably tend to break the capitalist mould which can no longer contain them, and these destroying principles are the elements of the new society.

"The historic mission of the class at present exploited, the proletariat, which is being organized and disciplined by the very mechanism of capitalist production, is to complete the work of destruction begun by the development of social antagonisms. It must, first of all, definitively wrest from its class adversaries the political power--the command of the force devoted by them to preserving intact their economic monopolies and privileges.

"Once in control of the political power, it will be able, by proceeding to the socialization of the means of production through the expropriation of the usurpers of the fruits of others' toil, to suppress the present contradiction between collective production and private capitalist appropriation, and to realize the universalization of labor, and the abolition of classes."[33]

If the "educated and professional" socialists cannot break the chain of this logic, they find themselves, as Nora did, face to face with the necessity of making a choice. Behind them is the old doll's house life with its manifold conventions--once useful, but through economic evolution outgrown and thus become false and deadly--a life, easy enough mayhap, but wholly devoid of idealism; before them is the new life of freedom, of revolt against outworn beliefs and conventions--a life of great difficulty, mayhap, but a life cheered by a noble ideal--an ideal in whose realization the socialist materialists believe as fully, as passionately as the ancient Hebrews believed in the fulfilment of the Messianic prophecies.

Theirs is a hard case. Without ideals they cannot, in any worthy sense, live. The only possible ideal, that even the keen eyes of so shrewd an observer as Mr. Street can perceive, is the ideal of Socialism. But they cannot accept this ideal without abandoning much, I do not say that is dear to them, but much that by habit and tradition has become part and parcel of their intellectual being.

If they decide to go forward into the New, the old world of dolls' houses must become a strange land to them. In the difficulties and trials of the new life, they cannot send back for aid to the old world, which will have become a world of strangers to them. Nora's woman's instinct did not fail her here; when Torvald asked if he could send help to her in case of need, her unhesitating reply was, "No, I say. I take nothing from strangers."

Far better is the case of the workingman attracted by the socialist ideal. The Nihilism of Socialism has no deterrent terrors for him, for, as Karl Marx said long ago, "he has nothing to lose but his chains, and a whole world to gain." He has long since lost all interest in religion; the factory by enlisting his wife and children as workers has already destroyed his home; and to him the State means nothing but the club of the policeman, the injunction of the judge, and the rifle of the militiaman.

But for the man of the "educated and professional classes" leaving the doll's house is indeed a difficult task. For its performance three things are requisite: a free and open mind, courage, and a vivid imagination. The Russian genius, Peshkoff (Maxim Gorky), did it, and did it with relative ease because he was a workingman before he became an educated man. For the same reason, though in a less degree, Jack London has also done it successfully, though here and there he still lapses into the doll's mode of thought. The sex-interest in the latter part of "The Sea Wolf" is obviously treated from the dolls' point of view; but it should be remembered that Mr. London necessarily expected the majority of the purchasers of "The Sea Wolf" to be dolls. But, in spite of this instance, we may be sure that Jack London brought but little with him when he left the Doll's House; and I am very sure he never sends back to have parcels forwarded to him.

When Mr. Upton Sinclair left the Doll's House, he evidently stuffed his mental pockets with a large assortment of intellectual lingerie and millinery from the doll wardrobes. In telling us what Life means to him in a recent magazine, he says that during a certain stress and storm period of his life he lived in close intimacy with three friends who "loved" him "very dearly." "Their names are Jesus, Hamlet and Shelley." Can any one imagine William Morris writing a sentiment so perfectly satisfying to a doll's sense of beauty? When I read these lines there rises before me a picture of the author tastefully robed in an exquisite dress--a doll's dress--of dotted swiss.[34]

Recently he has started a Co-operative Home Colony quite in the spirit of the bourgeois Utopians who founded Brook Farm more than half-a-century ago. Colony-founding, historians tell us, was a favorite amusement of the dolls of that era.

In the "Times Magazine" (for December 1906) he tells us that "the home has endured for ages, and through all the ages it has stayed about the same." This belief, I am informed, is almost universal among dolls.

I find myself the prey of a growing suspicion that Mr. Sinclair from time to time receives express parcels from the "Doll's House."

William Morris was a genius; he had a free and open mind; he had courage; and he had a vivid imagination. When he left the Doll's House, he took nothing with him, and he never afterward took anything "from strangers." It was his poet's imagination that enabled him to write "News from Nowhere," the only Utopia in whose communal halls the unwary reader does not stumble over dolls' furniture. Morris is the perfect type of the man of culture turned revolutionist.[35]

Mr. H. G. Wells has recently written a Utopian romance, "In the Days of the Comet," which, although it possesses in the fullest measure Mr. Wells' well known charm of style, is in substance at best a very feeble echo of "News from Nowhere." One of the modes of thought specially characteristic of eighteenth century French dolls is strongly to the fore in Mr. Wells' treatment of war. In the conversations "after the Change" between Melmount, the famous Cabinet Minister, and the pitiful, cowardly, inefficient hero (?), Leadford, they both appear to be inexpressibly shocked at the unreasonableness of war. It is true it is somewhat difficult to tell just what Melmount did think or feel, for Melmount is in one particular like Boston's distinguished litterateur, Mr. Lawson,--he appears to be constantly on the point of uttering some great thought, but never utters it. But so far as light is given us Melmount after the Change seems to have looked on war much as Carlyle did long before. Every one remembers Carlyle's two groups of peasants,[36] living hundreds of miles apart, who never heard of each other, and had not the slightest quarrel, the one with the other, but who none-the-less obeyed the orders of their respective kings, and marched until they met, and at the word of command shot each other into corpses. Most of us will agree with Carlyle and Melmount that, viewed from the peasants' standpoint, this was unreasonable to the point of sheer folly.

But, if I understand Mr. Wells aright, he seems to elevate the reason of the peasant into something very like the "eternal reason" of Diderot and Rousseau. He apparently forgets for the nonce that Engels long ago pointed out that "this eternal reason was in reality nothing but the idealized understanding of the eighteenth century citizen, just then evolving into the bourgeois." The difficulty that Mr. Wells will encounter in trying to bring human society into harmony with "eternal reason" is the impossibility of getting different classes of men to agree as to what is reasonable. No one outside of dolls' houses any longer believes in "eternal reason." Every man and every class has an ideal of what is reasonable, but these ideals vary. War is unreasonable to the peasant-target; it is also unreasonable to Melmount and Mr. Wells so far as they are representatives of the citizens of the classless society of the future, a society based on social solidarity, on world-wide brotherhood. But to the socialist materialist, war, in a world based on private ownership of the means of production used to produce commodities, with its concomitants, the wage-system, competition--domestic and international,--and ever-recurring "over-production," is so very far from unreasonable that it is absolutely inevitable.[37]

Mr. Wells evidently brought something with him when he left the Doll's House.

We now begin to realize what a very difficult matter it is to rid the mind completely of the effects of what Professor Veblen calls "the institutional furniture handed down from the past." The man, who yields to the lure of Socialism, must sooner or later effect a revolution within his own mind; if he does not, he will sooner or later return to his Doll's House, or make an excursion into some field of "pragmatic romance" where he will build himself a new doll's house.

Granted the truth of historical materialism, how will future generations look on the literature of to-day and yesterday? To a generation wholly untrained in theological, metaphysical and dualistic modes of thought how much meaning will there be in the poetry of Tennyson and Browning? For my part, I never read Browning now without being unpleasantly reminded of the aphorism Nietzsche put into the mouth of Zarathustra: "Alas, it is true I have cast my net in their (poets') seas and tried to catch good fish; but I always drew up the head of some old God."

But I am glad to believe that the matchless melody and the chiseled beauty of Tennyson's verse will charm the senses of men to whom his curious mixture of pantheism and Broad Church theology, which the middle classes of England and America in the latter decades of the nineteenth century welcomed as the ultimate massage of philosophy, will not be ridiculous only because it will be meaningless. But I am unable to think of the men of the future deriving any pleasure from our greatest poet, Browning. On the other hand it is not impossible that the fame of Swinburne will stand higher in the twenty-first century than it does in this opening decade of the twentieth.

The men and women of the future will, I am sure, feel themselves akin to Shelley. They will probably enjoy Byron too, so far as they understand him; but men and women, who have never known any relationship between the sexes but that of independence and equality, will be bored and baffled by that great bulk of Byron's verse which shocked his contemporaries.

When we turn to the drama, it appears probable that the revolution in the relations of the sexes will convert into mere materials for the historian even our greatest plays, such as Ibsen's "The Doll's House," Sudermann's "The Joy of Living," Maeterlinck's "Monna Vanna," and Shaw's "Mrs. Warren's Profession."

Are the "educated and professional" socialists prepared to accept gladly such tremendous changes? They are confronted by a momentous question. It was of their class William Morris was thinking when he wrote:

"I have looked at this claim by the light of history and my own conscience, and it seems to me so looked at to be a most just claim, and that resistance to it means nothing short of a denial of the hope of civilization.

This, then, is the claim:--

It is right and necessary that all men should have work to do which shall be worth doing, and be of itself pleasant to do: and which should be done under such conditions as would make it neither over-wearisome nor over-anxious.

Turn that claim about as I may, think of it as long as I can, I cannot find that it is an exorbitant claim; yet again I say if Society would or could admit it, the face of the world would be changed; discontent and strife and dishonesty would be ended. To feel that we were doing work useful to others and pleasant to ourselves, and that such work and its due reward could not fail us! What serious harm could happen to us then? And the price to be paid for so making the world happy is Revolution."[38]

Are they willing to pay the price? Nora paid the price for her freedom and paid it in full.

She took nothing from strangers.

If they are unwilling to pay the price, what is there left for them save the joyless sensuality and black despair of pessimism?

FOOTNOTES:

[7] "The Theory of Business Enterprise," Veblen, New York, 1904. Pages 351, 352. See also my article on Veblen the Revolutionist, International Socialist Review, June, 1905, vol. V, page 726.

[8] Throughout this article "nihilism" is not used in its strict technical or philosophical sense, but is used simply as a convenient term by which to designate the aggregate of those aspects of Socialism which, viewed from the standpoint of the existing regime, appear as negative and destructive.

[9] "A Contribution to the Critique of Political Economy." Karl Marx, New York, 1904. Pages 11, 12.

[10] "See Philosophical Essays," Joseph Dietzgen, Chicago, 1906. Pages 174

and 52.

[11] "Essays on the Materialistic Conception of History." Antonio Labriola, Chicago, 1904. Pages 85, 86.

[12] l. c. pages 155-6, 158.

[13] "Philosophical Essays." Dietzgen. Page 86.

[14] "Socialism and Modern Science." Enrico Ferri, New York, 1904. Pages 60, 61.

[15] "Philosophical Essays." Dietzgen. Page 116.

[16] The reader will observe that Ferri reads into the Erfurt pronouncement on religion (quoted in full above) a broader spirit of tolerance than its words necessarily imply.

[17] See "The Theory of the Leisure Class." Thorstein Veblen, New York, 1905. Pages 287, 288.

[18] Marx in "Zur Kritik der Hegelschen Rechts Philosophie."

[19] "The Origin of the Family, Private Property and the State." F. Engels, Chicago, 1905. Page 99, and "Woman under Socialism," August Bebel, New York, 1904. Page 127.

[20] Engels, "Origin of the Family, &c." Page 100.

[21] (Mrs. Parsons'.) The enlightened public opinion of to-day finds the chief if not the only warrant for universal male suffrage in its being an educational means. In this view women need the suffrage at present even more than men.

[22] (Mrs. Parsons'.) Dr. Alice Drysdale Vickery gave striking expression to

one phase of this subject at a recent discussion of the London Sociological Society. She urged that without economic independence the individuality of woman could not exercise that natural selective power in the choice of a mate which was probably a main factor in the spiritual evolution of the race. The American Journal of Sociology, Sept., 1905. Page 279.

[23] (LaMonte's.) No wonder such a startling hypothesis aroused the ire of our clerical friends.

[24] (LaMonte's.) It is worthy of note that this suggestion of a serious modification of marriage under existing economic conditions comes characteristically, not from a Socialist, but from the wife of a Republican member of Congress and the daughter of a distinguished financier.

[25] (Mrs. Parsons'.) Through the discovery of certain and innocuous methods of preventing conception. The application of this knowledge would have to be encouraged by public opinion in cases where conception would result in a degenerate offspring. Public opinion would also have to endorse the segregation of persons tainted with communicable sexual disease.

[26] Berlin cablegram in the New York Sun of Dec. 7, 1906.

[27] "Origin of the Family, &c.," Pages 91, 92. See also Bebel, "Woman under Socialism," Page 122, and elsewhere.

[28] "Origin of the Family &c." Pages 208, 209.

[29] On the existence of organized societies without a co-ercive State, see also, "Ancient Society." Lewis H. Morgan, Chicago, 1907.

[30] "Origin of the Family &c." Pages 211, 212.

[31] "Socialism: Utopian and Scientific." F. Engels, Chicago, 1905. Pages 76, 77.

[32] "The Economic Interpretation of History." Edwin R. A. Seligman, New York, 1903. Pages 105 and 109.

[33] "The People's Marx." Gabriel Deville, New York, 1900. Pages 18, 19.

[34] Cartoonists are warned that this idea is protected by copyright.

[35] The other day I chanced upon a pamphlet by one Oscar Lovell Triggs of Chicago. It bore the title, "William Morris, Craftsman, Writer and Social Reformer." In turning over its pages I was somewhat startled to read: "'Scientific' socialism he never understood or advocated." And again further on my eye fell on this gem: "It is apparent that Morris's 'Socialism' is poetic and not scientific socialism." This pamphlet should have a place of honor in every doll's library.

[36] In "Sartor Resartus."

[37] In fact, Professor Veblen has shown that for the last quarter of a century the commonest cause of seasons of "ordinary prosperity" has been war. See "The Theory of Business Enterprise." Pages 250-1.

[38] From "Art and Socialism," a pamphlet that is now rare.

THE BIOGENETIC LAW

It is very easy to go too far in drawing analogies between biology and sociology. Society--as yet, at least--is not an organism in the sense that a tree or a mammal is. It is quite true that with the perfect organization and solidarity to which Socialists look forward the analogy will be more complete than it is to-day, but for the present we must always remember that, as the lawyers would say, "the cases are not on all fours." If we bear these reservations in mind laws drawn from natural science are often of the greatest aid in enabling us to understand the phenomena of psychology and sociology.

One of the most helpful of these laws of science is the biogenetic law which is always associated with the great name of Ernest Haeckel, its most distinguished exponent. Doctor William B 鰈 sche, in his book[39] on Haeckel, uses, to illustrate this law, the familiar example of the frog. The mother frog lays her eggs in the water. In due course a new little frog develops from each of these eggs. But the object that develops from them is altogether different from the adult frog. This object is the familiar fish-like tadpole. It finally loses its tail, develops legs, and becomes a frog. Doctor B 鰈 sche discusses the matter as follows:--

"There are reasons on every hand for believing that the frogs and salamanders, which now stand higher in classification than the fishes, were developed from the fishes in earlier ages in the course of progressive evolution. Once upon a time they were fishes. If that is so, the curious phenomenon we have been considering really means that each young frog resembles its fish ancestors. In each case to-day the frog's egg first produces the earlier or ancestral stage, the fish, it then develops rapidly into a frog. In other words, the individual development recapitulates an important chapter of the earlier history of the whole race of frogs. Putting this in the form of a law, it runs: each new individual must, in its development, pass rapidly through the form of its parents' ancestors before it assumes the parent form itself. If a new individual frog is to be developed and if the ancestors of the whole frog stem were fishes, the first thing to develop from the frog's egg will be a fish and it will only later assume the form of a frog.

"That is a simple and pictorial outline of what we mean when we speak of the biogenetic law. We need, of course, much more than the one frog-fish before we can erect it into a law. But we have only to look around us and we find similar phenomena as common as pebbles.

"Let us bear in mind that evolution proceeded from certain amphibia to the lizards and from these to the birds and mammals. That is a long journey, but we have no alternative. If the amphibia (such as the frog and the salamander) descend from the fishes, all the higher classes up to man himself must also have done so. Hence the law must have transmitted even to ourselves this ancestral form of the gill-breathing fish.

"What a mad idea, many will say, that man should at one time be a tadpole like the frog! And yet--there's no help in prayer, as Falstaff said--even the human germ or embryo passes through a stage at which it shows the outlines of gills on the throat just like a fish. It is the same with the dog, the horse, the kangaroo, the duck mole, the bird, the crocodile, the turtle, the lizard. They all have the same structure.

"Nor is this an isolated fact. From the fish was evolved the amphibian. From this came the lizard. From the lizard came the bird. The lizard has solid teeth in its mouth. The bird has no teeth in its beak. That is to say, it has none to-day. But it had when it was a lizard. Here, then we have an intermediate stage between the fish and the bird. We must expect that the bird embryo in the egg will show some trace of it. As a matter of fact, it does so. When we examine young parrots in the egg we find that they have teeth in their mouth before the bill is formed. When the fact was first discovered, the real intermediate form between the lizard and the bird was not known. It was afterwards discovered at Solenhofen in a fossil impression from the Jurassic period. This was the archeopteryx, which had feathers like a real bird and yet had teeth in its mouth like the lizard when it lived on earth. The instance is instructive in two ways. In the first place it shows that we were quite justified in drawing our conclusions as to the past from the bird's embryonic form, even if the true transitional form between the lizard and the bird were never discovered at all. In the second place, we see in the young bird in the egg the reproduction of two consecutive ancestral stages: one in the fish gills, the other in the lizard-like teeth. Once the law is admitted, there can be nothing strange in this. If one ancestral stage, that of the fish, is reproduced in the young animal belonging to a higher group, why not several?--why not all of them? No doubt, the ancestral series of the higher forms is of enormous length. What an immense number of stages there must have been before the fish! And then we have still the amphibian, the lizard, and the bird or mammal, up to man.

"Why should not the law run: the whole ancestral series must be reproduced in the development of each individual organism? We are now in a position to see the whole bearing of Haeckel's idea."

In analogy with this, is it not true that every thinking man and woman in the course of his or her development, epitomizes the history of human thought? To be more specific, I take it that you, reader, are an educated man of middle-class origin, and that you have been a socialist for at least six months, and have, of course, read Engels' "Socialism: Utopian and Scientific." Now, is it not a fact that your socialism has developed from Utopia toward Science exactly along the lines Engels has traced for the movement at large? So true was this in my case that for a long time I was inclined to push the biogenetic law too far and to conclude that every socialist had traveled the same road. I still think the law holds here, but not in the narrow way I first applied it.

In the course of my work as an agitator (and socialist agitation is the best School of Socialism) I met many sterling socialists who had never been Utopians as I had. They were born fighters, so to speak, and had been full of the class spirit, and fighting the capitalists in the trade-union and elsewhere in every way they could think of, long before they had ever heard of the ideal of the Co-operative Commonwealth. And these men are among our best and most uncompromising socialists. Here was a hard problem for me. I believed in my law, but it did not seen to cover the cases of these militant socialists. I was long in solving the problem, but I solved it at last.

Socialism has two aspects. As the most vital fact of modern life it is a kinetic force. "Modern Socialism" in Engels' words "is, in its essence, the direct product of the recognition on the one hand, of the class antagonisms, existing in the society of to-day, between proprietors and non-proprietors, between capitalists and wage-workers; on the other hand, of the anarchy existing in production." This is Socialism, the most pregnant actuality in the palpitating life all about us. But, as Engels pointed out, Socialism also has its ideological side. In this sense it may correctly be called a theory, if we bear in mind that it is the virile force of class-feeling, and not the theory, that is going to effect the Social Revolution. Now, every individual socialist does in his development conform to the biogenetic law; but the bourgeois socialist is more apt to epitomize the history of Socialist theory, while the proletarian socialist recapitulates the development of class feeling as a kinetic force from blind and often unavailing hatred of the rich to the fruitful class-consciousness of the Marxian Socialist. The individual may combine these two processes in varying proportions; but in broad outline the bourgeois may be expected to reproduce fairly closely the history of Socialism, as a theory, while the proletarian reproduces the history of Socialism, the great kinetic force.

While, from the standpoint of socialist theory, the statement of Doctor Parkhurst and many others that "Christ was a Socialist" is a manifest absurdity, the historian who traces back the history of Socialism, the kinetic force, will surely be led by the chain of facts to James and Jesus and Isaiah. For they were among those who gave most effective expression to the class hatred which is the lineal ancestor of Marxian Socialism viewed as a kinetic actuality. In this sense Jesus was one of the founders of Socialism.

Here are a few extracts from these ancient sowers of the seeds of discontent:

"The Lord will enter into judgment with the ancients of his people, and the princes thereof: for ye have eaten up the vineyard; the spoil of the poor is in your houses.

What mean ye that ye beat my people to pieces, and grind the faces of the poor? saith the Lord God of hosts."

"Wo unto them that join house to house, that lay field to field, till there be no place, that they may be placed alone in the midst of the earth!" ISAIAH.

"Verily I say unto you, That a rich man shall hardly enter the kingdom of heaven.

And again I say unto you, It is easier for a camel to go through the eye of a needle, than for a rich man to enter into the kingdom of God."

"Wo unto you, scribes and Pharisees, hypocrites! for ye devour widows' houses, and for a pretense make long prayer: therefore ye shall receive the greater damnation." JESUS.

"Go to now, ye rich men, weep and howl for your miseries that shall come upon you.

Your riches are corrupted, and your garments are moth-eaten.

Your gold and silver is cankered; and the rust of them shall be a witness against you, and shall eat your flesh as it were fire. Ye have heaped treasure together for the last days.

Behold, the hire of the labourers who have reaped down your fields, which is of you kept back by fraud, crieth; and the cries of them which have reaped are entered into the ears of the Lord of Sabaoth." JAMES.

James would appear to have been somewhat more class-conscious than is deemed decorous by most of our modern Christian Socialists. But Isaiah and Jesus and James all give expression to precisely the same fierce emotions that I have many a time seen blazing out of the eyes of poor hopeless proletarians grouped around the soap-box; and it is the glory of Modern Socialism that it has been able to transform this fierce class hatred into intelligent class-consciousness which aims by loyalty to the Proletariat to rescue the rich as well as the poor from the fatal curse of economic inequality.

The bourgeois and the proletarian who come into the Socialist movement both have tadpole tails to lose in the course of their development into scientific socialists; but the tails are different. The proletarian has to rid himself of his hatred of the rich as individuals. He has to learn that Rockefeller, just as much as he himself, is a product of economic conditions. After he once thoroughly learns this there will be no danger of his being a Democrat or Anarchist or any other species of dangerous reactionary. The bourgeois tail is harder to lose. It consists of animistic, theological and dualistic habits of thought, issuing in utopianism and non-materialistic idealism. For, if I may be permitted to toy with the Hegelian dialectic in the manner of Marx, no man can be a fruitful idealist until he has become a materialist.

The reader of this volume will probably find himself able to agree pretty fully with what I have said in "Science and Socialism." That is because, when I wrote that, I had not fully gotten rid of my idealistic tadpole tail. He will probably have more difficulty in assenting to the theses of "The Nihilism of Socialism." That is because he has not yet gotten rid of his tadpole tail. I do not wish to be understood as speaking with contempt or depreciation of the tadpole tails. Without their aid most of us bourgeois socialist frogs would never have been able to get out of our old conservative shells. It was the utopianism of our tails, in most cases, that first cracked the shell.

I should be sorry to have any reader interpret the materialism of "The Nihilism of Socialism" into a disposition to deny or depreciate the great and beneficent influence that Christianity has had in the past. I should be greatly chagrined to be accused of irreverence in discussing religion. Irreverence is ever a sign of a narrow intellectual horizon and a limited vision. The scoffer is the product of the limited knowledge characteristic of what Engels called "metaphysical materialism." Unfortunately the mental development of many in the past has been arrested at this Ingersoll-Voltaire stage. But with the growth of Modern Socialism the tendency is for the metaphysical materialist to grow into socialist or dialectic materialism with its Hegelian watchword, "Nothing is; every thing is becoming."

The socialist materialist realizes that the obsolescent ideals of Christianity and the Family have played leading roles in the great drama of human progress. It is impossible for him to speak lightly or contemptuously of the ideals which have sustained and comforted, guided and cheered countless hosts of his fellows through the long, dark ages of Christian Faith. But he knows that those ages are past and that present day adherence to the old ideals is atavistic and reactionary. But none-the-less his mental attitude toward the old ideals is one of reverent sympathy and, I had almost added, gratitude. This state of feeling has found perfect expression in these lines by William Morris:

"They are gone--the lovely, the mighty, the hope of the ancient Earth: It shall labor and bear the burden as before that day of their birth; It shall groan in its blind abiding for the day that Sigurd hath sped, And the hour that Brynhild hath hastened, and the dawn that waketh the dead; It shall yearn, and be oft-times holpen, and forget their deeds no more, Till the new sun beams on Baldur, and the happy sea-less shore." (From SIGURD the VOLSUNG.)

FOOTNOTE:

[39] Haeckel: His Life and Work. By William Bosche. George W. Jacobs & Company.

KISMET.

"Verily I say unto you. That there be some of them that stand here which shall not taste of death, till they have seen the kingdom of God come with power." Mark, ix, 1.

The very close analogy between primitive Christianity and Modern Socialism has often been pointed out both by materialists, such as Enrico Ferri, and by Churchmen, such as the Reverend Doctor Hall.

We find in both the doctrine of the Advent. The primitive Christian believed in all simplicity and sincerity that he should not taste death until the Son of Man had come and established upon earth His kingdom of justice, peace and brotherhood. The Marxian Socialist to-day is even more sure that men and women now living will bear a part in the Social Revolution which is to usher in the reign of Fellowship on earth. The secret of the propaganda power of both movements is in the sincerity of this conviction.

Just at this point we are often met with two queries, both of which bear witness to the persistence of the utopian tadpole tails of the questioners. The first question is: If the early Christians were sincere and yet mistaken, may not the Socialists also be mistaken in their doctrine of the inevitability of Socialism? The second question is: If Socialism is inevitable--is coming anyhow--why do you Socialists vex your souls agitating for it?

The doubt of the inevitability of Socialism on analysis is always found to be a doubt of the pro-socialist desires and actions of the Proletariat. No one disputes that the Capitalist system is breaking down. With the great mass of the producers receiving bare subsistence wages the impossibility of disposing of the almost miraculously stupendous product of modern machines and processes is mathematically demonstrable. The former paradox of the Socialist agitator, that the Utopian is the man who believes in the possibility of the continuance of the present system, has become a platitude. Nor can many be found to dispute the statement that the centralization of industry in the United States has reached a point where Socialism is economically entirely practicable. The doubt of the sceptics is: Will the workers create, in the language of economics, an effective demand for Socialism? Two eminent Utopians have voiced this doubt in the recent past. Their names are George D. Herron and Daniel DeLeon. Both alike forget that the desires, ideals, and motives of the proletariat cannot but be in harmony with their economic environment, and I do not think that either of them would deny that, as we near the downfall of Capitalism, the economic environment will more and more imperatively drive men to Socialism as the only avenue of escape from chaos and pessimism. On this point, of the motives to action of the individual being formed by economic conditions, Marx wrote in "The Eighteenth Brumaire of Louis Bonaparte": "On the various forms of property, on the conditions of social existence, there rises an entire superstructure of various and peculiarly formed sensations, illusions, methods of thought and views of life. The whole class fashions and moulds them from out of their material foundations and their corresponding social relations. The single individual, in whom they converge through tradition and education, is apt to imagine that they constitute the real determining causes and the point of departure of his action." (Prof. Seligman's translation.)

The man who has thoroughly assimilated the doctrine of historical materialism cannot for a moment doubt the inevitability of Socialism. The utopianism which evinces itself in this doubt may be depended upon to betray itself elsewhere in the views of the doubters. We find that this is signally true in the case of the two illustrious utopian sceptics I have mentioned. The Natural Rights platform that Professor Herron wrote and the Socialist Party adopted in 1904 is only less utopian than Daniel DeLeon's curiously childish conceit that in the highly factitious, "wheel of fortune" form of organization of the Industrial Workers of the World[40] we have the precise frame-work of the coming Co-operative Commonwealth.

It does not seem too much to say that doubt of the inevitability of Socialism is in all cases a symptom of failure to apprehend clearly the full implications of the Materialist Conception of History.

The second question, If Socialism is inevitable, why do Socialists work to bring it about?, would appear to have been answered by implication in the course of our discussion of the first question. In brief, we work for it because we know that if we did not it would never come. It is inevitable simply because Socialists are inevitable. Our activity as Socialist agitators is a necessary result of the development of capitalist industry just as much as the Trust is. Again, we work for Socialism because we know we can get it, and we work all the harder if we believe it is coming soon. One of the most active of our wealthy socialists has said: "If I had to be in 'the hundred year, step at a time, take-what-you-can-get' class, you would find me automobiling my life away down at Newport with Reggie Vanderbilt instead of editing this magazine.... As said, I would rather chase down the pike on my Red Dragon at 'steen hundred miles an hour, terrifying the farmers, than go in for any 'reform game'." (Gaylord Wilshire in Wilshire Editorials. New York, 1907. Pages 232, 233.) So we find that in practice the belief in the inevitability and the proximity of Socialism is the most powerful stimulus to socialist activity.

We believe that the doctrine of the inevitability of Socialism is scientifically true, that its proclamation is the most effective weapon in the arsenal of the Socialist agitator, and that it is the most powerful incentive to Socialist activity; so that we mean exactly what the words imply when we address our non-socialist friends in the words of William Morris:

"Come, join in the only battle wherein no man can fail, Where whoso fadeth and dieth, yet his deed shall still prevail."

FOOTNOTE:

[40] I trust that no one will construe this as an attack on the Industrial Workers of the World. It is not my intention to express in this place any opinion as to the merits or demerits of that organization. It is only mentioned here because mention of it was necessary to illustrate the most curious case I know of the abnormally prolonged retention of the utopian tadpole tail.

www.ingramcontent.com/pod-product-compliance
Lightning Source LLC
Chambersburg PA
CBHW062018280526
45787CB00005B/2153